Contents

FOREWORD

Of all the distortions of scripture—and heaven knows there have been plenty in our time—the most disastrous is surely to suggest that when our Lord insisted that his Kingdom was not of this world, he meant that it was. An equivalent distortion would be to devise a version of the third temptation in the wilderness whereby our Lord, instead of rejecting the devil's offer of the kingdoms of the world, accepted it with a view to setting up an earthly paradise in accordance with contemporary specifications—some super-People's Democracy, or welfare state, or co-operative common-wealth. Harry Blamires' assault on this gerrymandering of scripture, and of Christian doctrine as it has come down to us through the centuries of Christendom, is a comfort and joy, more particularly since the contrary assumptions, put over by the media so assiduously and effectively, have come to be taken as irrefutable.

As a professional communicator—what St. Augustine called a vendor of words—I stand amazed at what has been done in the way of establishing what amounts to a humanistic, materialistic orthodoxy, called the consensus, and acceptable to young and old at all cultural levels. The consensus speaks, and none presume to contradict or even question its pronouncements, even though, as Mr. Blamires shows pungently and conclusively, more often than not they are intrinsically contradictory and nonsensical. How envious, I have often reflected, must Torquemada be, assuming he is in a position to observe our human scene, at so apparently effortless and painless an enforcement of consensus orthodoxy by comparison with his own laborious efforts with rack and thumb-screw and auto-da-fé, to achieve a similar result on behalf of the Church's orthodoxy.

Ever since life extricated itself from primeval slime, the consensus tells us, and began to evolve, steady progress was registered, until in due course, *homo sapiens*, or Man, arrived on the scene—an event described by the late J. Bronowski in his enormously popular and influential television series, *The Ascent of Man*, with singular fatuity as a sort of anthropological non-event:

> There is now a blank in the fossil record of five to ten million years. Inevitably, the blank hides the most intriguing part of the story, when the hominid line to Man is firmly separated from the line to modern apes. But we have found no unequivocal record of that, yet . . . . .

I like very much the use in the above quotation of the words "inevitably" and "yet"; language has, fortunately, a built-in propensity to reveal its own chicanery. Anyway, however Man did manage to come into existence, once in the world, according to the consensus, he went on progressing, though admittedly with occasional setbacks, until he reached the Enlightenment. Thenceforth, he was on his own, with no need to bolster himself up with transcendental aspirations, or to seek comfort in supernatural happenings or superstitious expectations.

It is comforting to note that throughout this fantasy account of Man progressing, there have been dissident voices, as Mr. Blamires' is today. For instance, in the seventeenth century, Pascal's, the more impressive because he was recognized as the most brilliant intellect and scientist of his time, whose splendid apologia for the Christian faith, his *Pensées*, has continued to instruct and uplift posterity as it did his contemporaries. Take the following passage, as apposite now as when it was written, if not more so:

> It is in vain, O men, that you seek within yourselves the cure for your miseries. All your insight only leads you to the knowledge that it is not in yourselves that you will discover the true and the good. The philosophers promised them to you, and have not been able to keep their promise. Your principal maladies are pride, which cuts you off from God, and sensuality which binds you to the earth; and they have done nothing but foster at least one of these maladies. If they have given you God for your object, it has only been to pander to your pride; they have made you think you were like him, and resembled him by your nature. And those who have grasped the vanity of such a pretention

have cast you down into the other abyss by making you believe that your nature was like that of the beasts of the field, and have led you to seek your good in lust, which is the lot of animals.

So we come to today, with consensus Man convinced that he is in a position to create his own kingdom of heaven on earth; seeing himself as in no wise dependent on what a number of contemporary clergy and theologians have described as "the myth of God incarnate" — meaning thereby the Incarnation, nor requiring a Church to formulate his beliefs, define his *mores* and provide his worship; seeing himself, indeed, in the unfortunate phrase of Dietrich Bonhoeffer, as having come of age, able to stand on his own feet, and dismiss the notion of sin as outmoded and the categories of Good and Evil as simplistic and unnecessary. Consensus man, that is to say, considers that he is moving triumphantly toward new dimensions of freedom — toward sexual freedom whereby, thanks to the birth pill, abortion, and easy divorce, he can indulge his carnal appetites without let or hindrance; toward economic freedom whereby, thanks to technological advances and an ever-rising Gross National Product, he can get more and more prosperous on less and less work; toward artistic and intellectual freedom whereby, with all the old taboos discarded, and unrestricted by considerations of sense or censorship or taste, he may eagerly follow up every new idea and new fashion of thought and expression, like the Athenians in the Apostle Paul's time, who cared about nothing else "but either to tell or to hear some new thing."

Mr. Blamires subjects all this burgeoning of the ego and proliferating of the appetites to a searching and devastating analysis, showing once again, as Pascal did more than three centuries ago, that without God and without the deliverance of the Incarnation, the freedom of Man Incarnate turns out to be only a new servitude, more terrible than any experienced before. What is conceived as a garden suburb turns out to be a Gulag Archipelago, and the mind that eschews belief in God, instead of believing in nothing, believes in anything.

As an experienced and discerning teacher, Mr. Blamires understands with particular clarity how barren and desolate is a mind self-restricted to mental data; how meager is the range of a pilgrim confined to Time, with no concept or sight of Eternity; how paltry is a vision that ends on the horizon. He sees and explains—helped thereto by the fortunate chance of having been a pupil and later a friend of C.S. Lewis—that the very vocabulary of our time is a devil's jargon, leading us to suppose that out of our earthly will can come heavenly dispositions, that here on earth our total destiny is worked out, that the clocks ticking on turn Now into Always. Whereas, actually, quoting C.S. Lewis, it is "in being as little as possible ourselves, in acquiring a fragrance that is not our own but borrowed, in becoming clean mirrors filled with the image of a face that is not ours," that we may truly realize ourselves. "Clean mirrors filled with a face that is not ours"—what a beautiful image that is!

In short, Mr. Blamires makes the essential point that "the Christian vocation is always to be a citizen of another kingdom, and therefore to live uneasily in the kingdom of this world." This was, he reminds us, St. Augustine's conclusion when he heard that Rome had been sacked; and we who are living in very similar circumstances to Augustine's, in order to keep our heads and save our souls, need to remember that here truly we have no continuing city, but that there is also the City of God which men did not build and cannot destroy, whose citizens we are of right, and whose citizenship runs for ever.

MALCOLM MUGGERIDGE

ACKNOWLEDGMENTS

This book contains some paragraphs used previously in lectures I delivered at the 24th Institute of Higher Education held by the United Methodist Church at Nashville, Tennessee in 1977, and other paragraphs used in the Colloquium at West Virginia Wesleyan College, Buckhannon, in 1978. It also contains material used in the H.I. Hester Lectures which I delivered at the Annual Meeting of the Association of Southern Baptist Colleges and Schools held at Asheville, North Carolina, in 1978, and which were subsequently printed in *The Southern Baptist Educator* (vol. XLII No 6 and vol. XLIII No 1). The passages in question are therefore associated in my mind with occasions on which I was privileged to enjoy American hospitality, with all that means of personal warmth and generosity: and I am deeply grateful to Dr. Fred Harris of the United Methodists and Dr. Ben Fisher of the Southern Baptists who were responsible for inviting me.

In other sections of the book I have drawn on two series of articles published in the London *Church Times* in Lent and in Autumn of 1978. Writing the articles, like preparing the American lectures, involved putting into shape ideas that would not otherwise have been articulated; and I am grateful to Bernard Palmer, the Editor of the *Church Times*, for commissioning them.

If Fred Harris, Ben Fisher and Bernard Palmer provided the initial stimulus for me to return to theological thinking, it was James Manney of Servant Books, Ann Arbor, who, by successfully re-issuing *The Christian Mind* and urging me to turn again to the issues it tackled with an eye on what has happened since it was written, impelled me to get to work on the book and make it what it is. To him I owe my sincerest thanks.

Introduction

WHERE DO WE stand? The question is intentionally ambiguous. In what kind of civilizational situation do we twentieth–century Christians find ourselves at this time? That is the first question and it calls for diagnosis. Where, in this present situation, thus defined and analyzed, must we twentieth–century Christians make a stand? That is the second question and it calls for prescription. The two meanings of the question are intertwined in such a way that it would be foolish to try to disentangle them for separate treatment in different sections of the book, diagnostic and prescriptive. As the book proceeds the emphasis moves this way and that; for logic bounces the argument like a tennis ball between the two sides of the net, between the question, What is our situation in the modern world? and the question, What ought we to do about it?

More specifically, the book examines the current interpenetration of Christianity and secularism, and the consequent need for the Christian to find the right footing for action. What bases of differentiated Christian commitment are necessary as footholds at a time when the flood of secularist propaganda would wash away the landmarks of all supernaturally-grounded allegiance?

I have used the words "diagnosis" and "prescription." They have a clinical connotation which reminds us that it is not always comforting to be told the truth. When a doctor defines the nature of cancer, that is interesting; when he detects a specific cancer and orders surgery, that is disturbing. There is safety and comfort in generalization in the religious and moral field as well as in the medical field. But the attempt to particularize can prove unpalatable. This applies especially to any attempt to define at what points Christian duty and the claims of this world are irreconcilable. We like to hear that the meek shall inherit the earth; we are less keen to

1

learn what individual changes we should have to undergo in character and status in order to qualify for inclusion among the meek. We may relish hearing of the spiritual perils of the rich; but we do not want to be told what maximum annual income we should have to be restricted to in order to be immune from those perils ourselves.

The conflict between the Church and the World, then, is one of those basic tenets of Christian teaching which are the more acceptable the less they are broken down and examined. If a writer sets out to characterize contemporary Western society as given over to materialism and self-seeking, he will find many people agreeing with him. If he sets out to define the Christian ideal of a society based on principles consonant with New Testament teaching, he will likewise find many people agreeing with him. But if he tries to locate precisely the actual points of antagonism between the society we live in and the ideal order whose ends we ought to serve, he will probably disturb a hornets' nest. We may be ready to hear contemporary civilization judged sharply for its self-indulgence and its decadence. We may be ready, if we are Christians, to hear the Christian virtues set forth as the only recipe for human welfare. But we are reluctant to have practical discrepancies between accepted daily attitudes and our Christian principles starkly itemized before our eyes. Dimly, at the back of our minds, we sense that the collision between worldly ends and the ends served on the Cross, if we expose ourselves to its full impact, will knock us off our accustomed footing in life.

Certain developments of the last twenty years have made the task of analysis in this field especially difficult. The substance of this book represents the accumulating reflections of some years on the fluid instabilities washing under the Christian's stance in the modern world. One cannot articulate such reflections without noting that not all those instabilities derive from the nature of current secularism. Some of them derive from the nature of recent theological thinking. Our present dilemma has to be examined against the background of an unsettled theological phase which has been sadly divisive within the Church itself and has consequently made doctrinal exposition more hazardous. It is too soon to say that this phase has run its course, but it can be argued that fashionable

trends have changed sufficiently of late to give an equivalent up-
dating of the orthodox case a new cogency. There remains a particular difficulty derivative from the general theological unrest, and
that is the extent to which the social gospel now dominates the
minds of many Christians. Exhortations to remember that the faith
has to do with eternal welfare as well as earthly welfare may strike
zealous activists as a kind of treachery and cowardice before some
of the crying human needs of the day. It will be necessary during
the course of this study to refer repeatedly to these special difficulties, for they impinge at many points on the matter under review:
that of putting into its late twentieth century context the question
of what belongs to Christ and what to Caesar.

Those of us who, when we were young, heard stories of the
heroic martyrdoms of old, quietly congratulated ourselves that we
had not been born into a society like that of Nero's Rome. The
sharpening of the Christian challenge into a choice between burning incense to Caesar and being thrown to the lions was happily not
going to come our way. It always seemed to me, as a child, a stroke
of monstrous good luck to have been born into the twentieth century in a society where being a Christian was the accepted thing.

That good fortune must not be underestimated. But we have all
learned a lot since childhood. There may not be any physical peril
inherent today in Christian profession, at least for us in the west;
but the challenge of Caesar to Christ has not disappeared. Persecution by physical torture and death is not the only form of victimiza-
tion. There are still plenty of altars to deified earthly authority on
which we are expected to throw incense. The conflict between the
Church and the World, between Christ and Caesar, will not go
away and cannot be resolved by shuttle diplomacy, however patient and protracted. The Christian's vocation is always to be a citizen of another kingdom and therefore to live uneasily in the kingdoms of this world.

Our Lord assured us that it was appropriate to pay tax to Caesar
in the coinage which bore his image and superscription. Bloody
martyrdoms soon afterwards witnessed how improper it was to
pay Caesar the homage due only to God. Somewhere along the line
between paying tax and throwing incense before the imperial bust
lay a frontier marking off permitted acquiescence in the world's

ways from unthinkable apostasy. It lies there still. The purpose of this study is to locate that frontier — or rather it is to induce the kind of clear-sightedness which will enable us to recognize the frontier when we stumble upon it in our daily wanderings. Nothing is easier than to cross it unthinkingly. For today's boundary between Christian fidelity and treachery is no floodlit Berlin wall, set about with watch-towers and man-traps, and patrolled by jealous guardsmen; it is a frontier barely recognizable on the terrain over which it runs. To locate it, you have to consult a map; and reliable maps, alas, are not easy to come by. If they were, there would be less need for this book, which is essentially mapwork. It charts the terrain and endeavors to locate where we stand in relation to the dividing line between faithful Christian witness and apostasy.

1

Where do we stand at this point of history?

It is often said that the religious, like the civil, crisis of our day is a crisis of authority. Time was when we heard a good deal in Christendom about the authority of the Church, and to any Christian who really understands what "authority" (*not* "authoritarianism") means, the concept is an important one—so important that there will be full treatment of it in a later chapter. It may be argued that in so far as Christians lose their sense of the authority of the Church, they are likely to succumb to the authority of the World. In the absence of firm theological leadership, Christians tend to lose their doctrinal nerve in deference to the authority of the World, and we have the spectacle of Christian spokesmen eagerly striving to accommodate Christian beliefs and prescriptions to the needs and tastes of modern society. Not very long ago this seemed to be the drift of supposedly Christian thinking in influential circles. There was talk of man coming of age and being liberated, and of

5

the need for the Church to catch up with this grown-up marvel. But, in some quarters at least, there has been a change since then. Complacency with the achievements of our civilization has been dented; protest against our economic and industrial set-up and against global inequalities has become commonplace inside and outside the Church.

Sometimes a sentence remembered by chance will linger in the mind to represent a whole body of thought in microcosm. I remember attending a church conference back in 1964 when a clergyman (a Canadian) told me with some enthusiasm what delight he took in modern cities. "The sweep of the concrete overpasses," he said excitedly. "There's God for you. Isn't that right?" The sentence stayed in my mind through the years as summing up a theological phase in which the mood was one of Christian confidence in our secular civilization. It stays with me now as a reminder of how phases pass away.

For the mood of Christendom today is very different. The change has been vividly brought home to me as a result of my rather odd experience as a writer deeply engaged with theology in the 1950s and early 1960s and then exclusively preoccupied with other matters for some twelve years or so. Returning recently to the world of church conferences after this gap, I received the impact of the changed times with startling freshness. I found no one eulogizing contemporary urbanism. On the contrary, I found thoughtful people voicing their grave worries over the drift of our civilization in its social and technological aspects. One mother told me, with wry resignation, how her children were forcing their parents in conscience to shut off the heating and the air conditioning, to simplify diet, and to refrain from using the car, indeed to suffer considerable discomforts, and all in protest against America's excessive use of resources in an elsewhere needy world. The drift of this mother's lament appeared to be that the Church did not fully match up to the demands of the idealistic young in protest against a materialistic and self-indulgent society.

In reflecting on this conversation, I recalled that at a theological conference back in the mid 1960s there seemed to be a feeling among some clergy that Christian judgment upon the modern world was unwarranted, and that we ought perhaps to be hymning overpasses instead of cherubim and seraphim. Yet now, at a similar conference in the late 1970s, the disturbing question that came up, prompted by the behavior of the young, was whether perhaps Christian judgment upon the modern world did not go far enough; whether the Christian who did not turn off his heating system and leave his car in the garage was really a humanist in disguise.

There is indeed, both inside the Church and outside the Church (as much recent literature shows) less complacency with the state of our society than there was perhaps fifteen years ago. Not that secular skepticism about our civilization is by any means the same thing as Christian skepticism about it. The former tends to breed despair. The latter is rooted in hope, for it is grounded in awareness of God. The former issues in nihilistic literature of the absurd. The latter is productive of work and witness. Secular skepticism about the world is wholly negative, for it opens no doors and offers no comfort. It is one-track and one-eyed. Christian skepticism about the World is a by-product of faith and hope in another order that can itself transform this one. It is one half of a double-track commitment to God and to man; one prospect in a two-eyed view of this life and another one.

Secular disillusionment with the secular world is not of direct concern to this thesis, but, as a literary man, I have been much concerned with the state of mind revealed in the literature of our age. It has always seemed to me ironical that a movement toward secularization in the Church itself should have gathered momentum at a time when great writers were expressing a loss of confidence in the secular order. This has been one of the most remarkable features of the theological developments of the last few decades; that just when great writers on whom young intellectuals feed their minds in our universities were subjecting contemporary civilization and current secular values to a ruthless scrutiny, and pouring scorn upon aspects of our social and economic set-up, so-called Christian theologians started trying to adjust religious thinking to accommodate bankrupt secular criteria.

It is odd that the aberrant theologians of the trendy 1960s should have so wilfully lined themselves up with the philistines. One of the things that emerges most clearly from extensive study of twentieth–century English literature is that, time and again, high literary quality is linked with skepticism about the accepted values of our civilization—with skepticism about "the World." Yet these last two decades have seen supposedly eminent Christian theologians rushing to ally themselves with secular trends rejected by our thoughtful men of letters. It is symptomatic of this irony that in the very years when theologians were hailing the coming of age of liberated man, William Golding, the novelist, was quietly explaining to student audiences on American university campuses how the Second World War destroyed, at least for a time, his belief in the perfectibility of social man. "I believed then that man was sick—not exceptional man, but average man. I believed that the condition of man was to be a morally diseased creature....To many of you, this will seem trite, obvious and familiar in theological terms. Man is a fallen being. He is gripped by original sin. His nature is sinful and his state perilous. I accept the theology and admit the triteness; but what is trite is true..." So Golding wrote in the piece called *Fable*, printed in his collection of occasional pieces, *The Hot Gates* (1965). *Fable*, he explains in the Preface to the collection, dealt with aspects of his novel, *Lord of the Flies*, and was first used for a lecture at UCLA in California in 1962. "I elaborated this lecture and took it round a variety of American universities where it answered some of the standard questions which students were asking me."

Golding is not untypical of those intellectuals who were brought up on Wellsian rationalism and progressivism earlier in the century and then rejected it—not all of them, of course—in favor of a religious creed. Some of them indeed chose sheer nihilism, the philosophy of the absurd. Golding exemplifies a notable literary trend of his times. You will certainly not find among the really great imaginative writers of this century men or women formulating their prescriptions for the well-being of the human psyche within the framework of a materialistic technological society. You will have to turn to so-called theologians for that. The point can be reinforced by instances far more extreme than the case of William Golding. For in the years when aberrant theologians began extolling the creative potential newly on offer to post-Freudian liberated man, Samuel Beckett became perhaps the dominant literary figure of the time. Beckett represented modern man in terms of impotence. In novel after novel, play after play, he produced a series of disturbingly authentic studies of deprivation and immobility as his commentary on the human scene in the technological era. When the tide of current culture and social substance impinges upon the blank world of the two tramps in *Waiting for Godot*, it is in the form of a showy, empty-headed tyrant who drives a roped slave on all fours before him with a whip. The bluster of the master and the crazy rhetorical mishmash poured out by the slave clearly represent the most that contemporary civilization is likely to be able to provide in the way of answer to patient representatives of waiting humanity, rootless as they are, and bereft of dignity and meaningful purpose. If Beckett reiterates any significant comment on our day, it is that, over against the lostness, the alienation, the utter powerlessness of modern man, the noises that our civilization makes under the guise of rational utterance are void and irrelevant. The numerous verbal currencies that uphold our social and professional roles are shown up in all their absurd nullity. By contrast Beckett's first fictional hero, Murphy (in the novel, *Murphy*), has a mind which is not built "on the correct cash-register lines, as an indefatigable apparatus for doing sums with the petty cash of current events," and when he takes a post in a lunatic asylum he is consumed with esteem for the patients. He finds highly questionable the clinical treatment of those who are supposedly "cut off" from reality. Indeed his "experience as a physical and rational being obliged him to call sanctuary what the psychiatrists called exile and to think of the patients not as banished from a system of benefits but as escaped from a colossal fiasco."

The purpose here is not to recommend the view of current human civilization as a colossal fiasco, but to juxtapose this view, as an instance of the kind of thinking that taxed the minds of students in the 1960s (and still taxes them), with the trendy "theological" impetus that would have lined up Christians with the idolators of the modern secularized society.

The conflict between the Church and the World is always with us. The choice between serving God and Mammon always faces us. It will always be the Christian's duty to counter current acceptance of secularist criteria. You can set your heart only upon either things above or things beneath. For this reason the Christian evangelist is obviously not always, superficially speaking, the bearer of good cheer (though he is always the bearer of good tidings). He cannot be forever mouthing boosts to confidence. For if a man's heart is fixed on things beneath, you do him no unkindness by disturbing his complacency and drawing his attention to the frailty and instability of that to which he clings for happiness. When H.G. Wells referred to his agnostic uncertainties rather flippantly in a letter to G.K. Chesterton, Chesterton replied, "I should worry about it if I were you." I should worry about it. How often is the Christian response precisely that — a response of turning the usual secular advice upside down? Instead of: Don't worry about it, Do worry about it. One side of the Christian coin is the good news of the joy to be found in God's love. The other side is the assurance of how inadequate are all rival satisfactions.

If it is a prime Christian duty to shake people from their reliance upon secular criteria (as we should say today), from setting their hearts on things beneath (as our forefathers would have put it), then we should take note that the intellectual environment is not wholly unfavorable to our case. The instances I have cited — by drawing upon William Golding and Samuel Beckett — in their different ways illustrate the point. Distrust of current secular criteria is prevalent over fields of thought little touched by Christian thinking. If one were to try to represent by diagram the relationship of two bodies of people in our Western world — firstly, Christians; secondly, people who distrust secular criteria — we should find ourselves with two rectangles only partially overlapping. The grey area of overlap alone represents healthy thinking, for it represents Christians who reject dominant secularist philosophies. Of the two "white" areas, the one represents critics of the modern world who have no faith to give a positive meaning to their distrust and can therefore only resort to cynicism and despair. The other "white" area represents Christians who are trying to have it both ways, to worship God and Mammon together, to serve the kingdom of God and to acquiesce in the values of a hedonistic and materialistic society.

The fact that we find Christian teachers, clergy, and indeed so-called "theologians" in this area ought not to surprise us, though of course it must always sadden us. The struggle between the Church and the World has never been represented by clear-cut battle-lines and sharply differentiated groups of men and women. Indeed, in recent times, the danger to the Church from infiltration, from corruption by secularist worldliness from within, has perhaps been the dominant aspect of our struggle. There will be more to be said about this later; but meanwhile we may note a similar evolution in both the civil state and the Church. In the world of civil politics the struggle for wholesomeness and justice is ceasing to be fought out in external, that is international, warfare, and is beginning to be fought out in internal conflict — that is, disorder, protest, and rebellion within the individual state. Similarly, in the spiritual commonweal, the struggle for wholesomeness and godliness is ceasing to be fought out only in external conflict between the Christian and the rationalist, the humanist, and the secularist, and is increasingly fought out in internal conflict within the Christian body between Christians who have accepted the implications of their faith and Christians who are disguised rationalists, humanists, and secularists, unwittingly given over to the weakening of the divine body from within.

It is surely not fanciful to detect a connection between the national polity and the Church here. In respect of well-being or sickness, notable characteristics of the one match those of the other. If this is an age of inner unrest and indiscipline in the nation, it is certainly an age of unrest and indiscipline in the Church. It is also of course an age of individual unrest and indiscipline. It would seem that the polities of nation and Church alike, in a given age, are perhaps blessed and afflicted, in respect of well-being and of sickness, by notable characteristics that match those of the individual citizen or Churchman. The point is made because it appears that the ruddy individualistic strength of Victorian society, essentially ruthless and competitive, devoted to the survival and flourishing of the fittest at whatever economic and cultural cost in massive human waste and failure, was matched at the level of personal physical life by the widespread wasting disease of consumption and the prevalent wastefulness of high infant mortality and deformity. It is significant therefore that the characteristic personal ailments of our day should be mental disorientation and cancer. For in the life of man writ large in national society, the prevalent evils are disorientation of intellectual leadership and inner decomposition bred of excess rather than of deprivation. Similarly, in the life of Christian man writ large in the divine society, the Church, the prevalent evils are the mental disorientation represented by the decline of doctrinal and institutional authority, and the cancer represented by the inner proliferation of malignant secularism, humanism, and materialism that corrode the vitals of the Christian body.

As it is folly for a nation to imagine that its main enemy is outside when its culture, its morale, and its decencies, public and private, are being rotted from within, so it is folly for the Christian Church to imagine that its main enemy is open atheism when its creeds, its otherworldliness, and its essential forms and practices, public and private, are being undermined from within. It is time for Christians to face the realities of the present situation. When cancer is diagnosed, it is time for surgery.

Enough has now been said about the first point on which the opening thesis of this book hangs—the sense that perhaps there is thinking abroad more susceptible to the wholesale claims that the Christian message in its fullness makes vis-à-vis the social set-up of our day. We are perhaps readier to be told—and to hear with gratitude—that the kingdom is not of this world.

The second point on which these opening reflections are based derives from a personal experience quite outside the field of religious thought or action. It was one of those incidents which, slight at the time, linger in the memory, take root, acquire deeper and deeper meaning as the years pass, until eventually, in spite of the apparent insignificance of the initial event, they are transformed into symbols of deep meaningfulness in the memory, and are transmuted into signs of momentous change.

It happened in the world of higher education where I spent many years of my teaching life. The date was the late 1960s. A young lady in her twenties came to see me in connection with a proposed summer school. She was a personable and well-educated young woman, a highly articulate and intelligent graduate, and her post was one of considerable responsibility. It involved planning cultural courses in the United Kingdom for visiting students from American universities. When business was done, we began to talk about the educational world as educationists do. Some words she used, not immediately noted much, stuck in my mind and will now always stick there as pointing to a watershed in educational history, perhaps in cultural history. She spoke of her own school days. "I was lucky," she said. "I was educated under a backward county authority and came too soon for all the changes." The changes she was referring to were those of replacing our selective educational system by the undifferentiated comprehensive schools. It is not the purpose to argue here whether she was right or wrong. What stuck in my mind was the naturalness with which a young lady congratulated herself for having escaped the march of progress. Lucky to have been educated by a backward authority.

The point is that educated people can and do say now what would have been unthinkable 20, 30, 40, 50 years ago — and more; namely, that they are glad to have escaped what the young are now getting. Considered in cold blood, it is an astonishing admission for the educational system to have provoked. To anyone who was brought up in pre-war days, one of the firmest memories of early life is the assurance with which the older generation admired and envied the provisions made for the young. The constantly reiterated comment of the older generations in the 1920s and 1930s, when faced by the facts of the schooling provided for their children and their grandchildren was, "How wonderful! If only it had been like that in my day! Aren't they lucky!" Surely if there has been one constant over the last hundred years and more of public education — until the last decade — it has been the genuine envy of each generation of the educational provisions made for the next. From my schooldays onward I was conscious of my immense good fortune in having been educated, not under a backward, but under a progressive county authority which pioneered grammar-school education for all who seemed to merit it. And how parents and grandparents envied the educational provisions made for us.

Are we then, we who are now parents, the *first generation in the history of modern education* to look at our children's schooling and question honestly whether it is as good as our own was?

It begins to look like a turning point in history. The voice of that young lady has rung in my mind ever since she said those words. "I was lucky. I was educated under a backward authority." They have rung in my mind as I have sat in meetings where great decisions were being made in the perpetual tampering and tinkering with our educational system. They have rung in my mind as teachers, governors, educationists and the rest of them have waxed eloquent in committee over the ever-progressing movement toward comprehensivization, participation, open methods, group-this and group-that. Yes; but suppose at the end of it all we produce a whole series of generations of ex-pupils all echoing that young lady, all congratulating themselves for having missed the next batch of "improvements" being inflicted on their immediate successors!

A worrying aspect of our current situation is that it is the better-educated, more reflective and wiser among us who are the readiest to question current educational trends. There is no longer any eyebrow-raising in cultured circles when an intellectual begins to speak of the failure of mass education. The gap between educationists and men of culture has never been wider because the gap between education and culture has never been wider. Indeed a fundamental question at issue is precisely the relationship between education and culture. The severance of the two lies at the back of our ills.

Talk of the transmission of culture is rarely heard today, but in fact there can be no escape for an educational system from the duty to transmit culture from one generation to the next. If you teach a child to walk or to speak, you are involved in the transmission of culture. If you teach a child to wash its hands and to eat with a knife and fork, you are involved in the transmission of culture. Culture is everything that makes human life distinct from animal life and which nourishes practices that are not dictated by physical desire or necessity alone. Necessity requires a human being to get about, but not specifically on two legs and in an upright position. Necessity requires a human being to eat, but not specifically with clean hands and at a table.

It will be observed that the examples of the transmission of culture here cited, vital as they may be to health, hygiene, and civilized living, leave no room for current slogans of educationists. For none of these practices — to eat hygienically, to walk on two legs, to speak coherently — can be acquired without discipline. None of these represents a natural development. None of them could have been discovered unaided by pupils. None of them issues from a native fount of creativity in the child's individuality. None of them represents something which the child could possibly have consciously willed and wanted in advance of having them. This last is perhaps the most crucial point. For of all the fallacies dominating current thinking in the educational, the social, and indeed the religious field, none is more stubborn, yet more ill-founded, than the notion that human beings know what they want in advance of getting it — except in the very general sense that they want happiness, fulfillment, health, and peace of mind.

The pupil who has Latin nouns and verbs drummed into him in early childhood and struggles with the use of the subjunctive tenses in his early teens has no conception of the pleasure he will derive if he persists with the arduous toil until he can read Virgil's *Aeneid* for himself. If he is made objectively aware of such delight in store, it is something he must take wholly on trust from his teacher without any kind of surging subjective impulse or even responsive inner warmth. Indeed the whole process, if it is to be fruitful, takes place under the aegis of authority accepted and discipline submitted to. The pupil whose ear and mind are trained in childhood by aural tests and the study of musical structures like the sonata form has no conception of the pleasure he will derive if he persists with the practice of alert listening until he can explore the Beethoven symphonies in his twenties and the Last Quartets in his forties. Again, the whole process, if it is to be fruitful, takes place under the aegis of authority accepted and discipline submitted to.

Without submission to authority and discipline there is no culture; there is only sub-culture — the idle acceptance of the easily assimilable that bypasses understanding and lays its touch on the senses at their rawest. It is no accident that the age in which authority and discipline are increasingly discounted in religious and educational circles should be the age of the pop star, the telly-addict, the age of mindless wallowing, hour by weary hour, in stillborn verbal banalities tricked out with rhythmic and harmonic clichés of surpassing staleness and insipidity.

More will have to be said about authority in the course of this book. It is a key concept for anyone trying either to diagnose our current ills or to prescribe a remedy. For the moment, the subject is lightly touched upon because wider questions are at issue. Where is our culture going? A sentence casually spoken ten years ago has, in the years since, repeatedly made me wonder whether our educational system itself might have gone into reverse. Correspondingly I wonder whether this watershed reached in the matter of bringing up the young marks a turning point in human affairs in the Western world.

There are thoughtful people, quite outside the Church, who would say that it does. Charles Fair, in his book, *The New Nonsense* (1974), is much concerned with what he calls the "end of the rational consensus." Whether our crisis can be accurately defined as the end of a consensus seems to me to be doubtful. The word "consensus" implies mass agreement. The Victorians imposed on the nation an ethic of work, duty, piety and so on by force of the authority of institutions like the state, the educated élite, the bosses, and the aristocracy. It is doubtful whether the word "consensus" ought to be applied to popular practical acquiescence in a system whose precepts, values, and other rigidities the masses were too poor, enslaved, and powerless to question. If we are seeing the spread of a dispersed, discrete irrationality, it is not because a democratic "consensus" has come to an end, but because authority has been dislodged. The notion of consensus (which carries overtones of democratic expression of the popular will) is historically subsequent to a phase in which authority was acquiesced in. This may seem to be a quibble, but the intention here is to question whether one ought to characterize our present situation (in civil or religious matters) as one in which the people at large have changed their minds — opting for diversified nonsense in exchange for reason. If people at large (in the nation or in the Church) are succumbing to nonsense in place of reason, it is not because they have personally altered their opinions; it is because they are submitting to a new "authority" — or rather "anti-authority."

It is one of the paradoxes of the situation that anti-authority, which is irrational, is always authoritarian, while true authority, which is rational, is essentially anti-authoritarian. For anti-authority fills the vacuum left by the sucking away of authority. It must necessarily fill it with nonsense and banality, for positive culture and understanding, morality and decency, are inseparably bound up with authority and discipline. It would be nonsensical to use the word "authority" of, say, pop music or scientology, both of which are drugs numbing the sensitivities and putting the mind to sleep. The highly paid pop star or the prophet of a fake "religion" is not a molder of mind or taste, for he corrodes both; nor is he even a satisfier of legitimate appetite but an exploiter of unwariness and illiteracy. It is not wayward choice but the lack of choice that lies behind submission to pop music or scientology, for choice is rooted in intelligent awareness. Lack of choice means lack of freedom. That is why, ultimately, pop stars and cult leaders are more "authoritarian" in impact and influence than true authority can ever be. They enslave, and true authority never enslaves. It frees.

Be that as it may, it was a sentence in Charles Fair's book that brought my reflections about the educational and cultural watershed to a head. Speaking of the years subsequent to the twelfth-century days of Louis le Gros, Fair observes: "The process by which our tradition has slowly expanded in the centuries since, bringing increasing (if never very large) numbers of fully developed, rationally self-possessed individuals in its train, may now have begun to reverse itself."

Charles Fair's voice is not a Christian voice. I do not know whether the young lady whose lament about educational regress awakened this discussion was a Christian. Probably in neither of these cases are we faced by a specifically Christian judgment upon society. Yet these two judgments, implying that we have gone into reverse, are seized upon here as relevant starting points in a Christian diagnosis of contemporary society. In citing them, and recognizing that they are not Christian, we perhaps stumble upon a key to our dilemma. For surely organized Christianity presupposes civilization. It is preached and practiced effectively within an ordered polity. In a jungle, where cannibals dine on missionary stew, where men prey bestially upon one another, certain preliminary steps toward minimal restraint, hygiene, and the guarantee of continuing survival have to be taken before a prayer meeting can be arranged and the gospel proclaimed. Again, in a lunatic asylum where the saddest human cases are confined, the same conditions would apply before any homiletic topic could be usefully entered upon. In this sense organized Christianity presupposes civilization and it presupposes sanity. Our Lord's work was done within a province of the Roman Empire where the appurtenances and safeguards of civilized life were available. He was able to read, to argue in the temple, and, in his teaching, to use allusions and references that implied a residuum of knowledge in his hearers derived from their own culture and tradition. When our Lord came across the demons of inner disintegration — of raving madness — he expelled them from their habitations in human hearts and sent them plunging into the sea in the bodies of swine.

These points are made because we hear influential voices about us suggesting that civilization may have gone into reverse. The notion introduces an entirely new dimension into consideration of the Christian perspective. It may be too late to ask where we stand as Christians if the pressing need is to ask where we stand as civilized men (over against barbarism) or as rational men (over against mass lunacy). That is one way of putting my point. And paradoxically the other way of putting it is to reverse a crucial term. It may be too *soon* to ask where we stand as Christians if the pressing need is to ask where we stand as civilized men or as rational men. It may be too *late* to ask where we stand as Christians in the historical sense that we should have been watching our outer defences in order to protect our inner citidel. It may be too soon to ask where we stand as Christians in the logical sense that barbarism and lunacy will have to be expelled from the city before the citadel's authority can be reasserted within its walls. It may well be that the devils of barbarism and insanity have to be sent plunging into the sea before sermons can be preached on the mountains and the five thousand fed.

It was an odd coincidence (perhaps, if I were a man of sturdy faith, it would come naturally to me to write "an act of Providence" instead of "an odd coincidence") that caused me to pick up St. Augustine's *De Civitate Dei* in the same week that I read Charles Fair's attack on contemporary American civilization in *The New Nonsense*. "This," writes Sir Ernest Baker in his introduction to the book for the modern reader, "is what makes the work one of the great turning-points in the history of human destiny: it stands on the confines of two worlds, the classical and the Christian, and it points the way into the Christian." It may be that we too stand on the confines of two worlds, the Christian and the post-Christian. Certainly there are plenty of cultural agencies around us pointing the way into the post-Christian world. Augustine saw the Roman Empire collapsing around him. Rome was sacked by the Goths in 410, and Augustine set about proclaiming the immutability and stability of that heavenly city "which has truth for its king, love for its law, and eternity for its measure." For no writer in Christian history was the distinction between the Christian and the secular, the city of God and the city of this world, more agonizingly real.

But Charles Fair and his like would argue, not that we stand on the confines of two worlds, the Christian and the post-Christian, but that we stand on the confines of two worlds, the rational and the irrational, the rationally consensical and the irrationally non-sensical. And indeed the apparent coincidence of two such changes, or turning points, is what most essentially concerns us in this chapter, where an attempt is being made to disentangle specifically Christian worries from the worries of those who, without being Christians, knowingly prefer civilization to barbarism, virtue to vice, decency to moral squalor. For, desperate as we Christians are to stem the tide of immorality and degeneracy, we must not pretend that it is simply *qua* Christians that we man the barricades. It is an insult to paganism to suggest that it is only by virtue of our Christian conscience that we are offended by the collapse of morality and public decency. It is not just St. Paul, St. Augustine, John Bunyan or John Wesley who would be horrified at what we have come to acquiesce in the way of legalized embryonicide and pornography. Surely Virgil and Seneca, Plato and Plotinus would be horrified too.

Our problem is similar to, yet very different from, St. Augustine's. The barbarians had taken Augustine's imperial capital, and barbarians have taken over commanding metropolitan positions in our society — in our press, our broadcasting companies, our governments, our schools. Civilization is based on authority and order, peace and restraint, virtue and self-discipline. In so far as influential positions in our social systems are taken over by the apostles of anarchic self-assertiveness and self-opinionatedness, of clamor, disorder, conflict, and permissiveness, they are taken over by anti-civilizational agencies. Where authority and discipline are replaced by the anarchy of license—intellectual, emotional and physical—power falls into the hands of the barbarians. We have today at our disposal some of the most potent mind-molding instruments ever devised by man. Can we pretend that they are used, by and large, to recommend the life of virtue and self-discipline? It is not just a question of what is urged upon the young in our educational institutions as a pattern of the good life at a time when, as we shall see later, eccentric and amoral ideals of human integrity are widely canvassed among the intelligentsia. It is also a question of what models of satisfaction and self-fulfillment are set before us as we imbibe what is presented by the media and the advertisers.

The necessary function of advertisers in transmitting information about what is available in the way of commodities and amenities cannot be performed in an ideological vacuum. One cannot announce that bread is for sale without implying that bread is worth having. The presentation of information about goods and amenities cannot be insulated from qualifying undercurrents of approval or depreciation. Correspondingly the reflection of contemporary life in entertainment and documentation cannot be insulated from evaluative overtones that recommend or denigrate Thus an image of the good life is conveyed to us by the advertisers and the media, and, according to the measure of our intellectual and our spiritual resources, we accept it or we reject it.

The weaker among us succumb to allurements toward self-indulgence and to illusory dreams of self-aggrandizement; the weakest of all limp into bemused states of mingled aggression and lust, envy and discontent, protest and insanity. The values and propaganda of the less responsible media-men and advertisers fuel wage demands by filling workers with a lust for sharing in the indulgences apparently recognized as a part of the good life by the cheapjacks of the publicity game. No Christian exhortation and admonishment today can afford to ignore the media, for Christian teaching has to insist upon a set of values clean contrary to those in vogue in the media world which sets the standard of many people's thinking.

Notice what has just been said: that the media tend to set the standard of people's thinking. And ponder what that means. If the media set the standard for people's thought and behavior, then the media have become their *authority* for thought and behavior. That is what has happened, ironically enough. Christians and education-ists have been lifting up their hands in horror ar.d saying, "Oh no, no, no. We must not assert authority any longer. We cannot do with that kind of thing in our democratic age." And while Christians and schoolteachers have been talking like that, the media men have quietly substituted a new authority, which I prefer to call "anti-authority," because it asserts the negative standards of worldliness and permissiveness. Habits of thought and behavior are being adjusted to match a presentation of life as a sensual free-for-all from which moral imperatives have been shot away and spiritual reality banished.

The presence of barbarism at the heart of our polity and threading its venomous way through the veins of our culture gives our situation some comparability with St. Augustine's. If Augustine had to watch the collapse of a pagan order, we perhaps watch the collapse of the supposedly "Christian" order that superseded it. There is no need to remind readers that the so-called "Christian" civilization of the West, whose twilight we perhaps now observe, was never a civilization soaked through with Christian faith and commitment. At best it has been what we call a nominally Christian civilization. In short, if we speak of "Christian civilization" we speak of something much more widely diffused than real Christian faith and practice. And since real Christian faith and practice are much more difficult to measure than the spatial and temporal bounds of a supposedly Christian civilization, we cannot say how powerful the Christian core of commitment and practice has been in this age or that. It is important to remember this, because — for all the comminations that may appear to have been called down in these pages so far — there is no intention to make this a depressing or pessimistic book. And it may well be that what I have called "the Christian core of commitment and practice" is as strong today in our no longer ostensibly Christian civilization as it was in centuries when the term "Christian civilization" might have seemed to form a more accurate description of the state of society. Indeed it *could* be (I do not pretend to know) that Christian faith and practice are today more powerful in the world than ever—for they were never very powerful in overtly measurable terms. But "Christian civilization" has been riddled through with corruption, as our history books make clear.

So, if St. Augustine was watching the collapse of a pagan order, it would perhaps be fallacious to imagine that we, by contrast, are watching the collapse of a Christian order. Surely, if we are watching a collapse, it is rather that of a civilization which failed to take Christianity deeply into its system than one deeply imbrued with Christian faith and practice. If we stand on the confines of two worlds, those worlds can perhaps better be described as the allegedly Christian and the frankly non-Christian than as the Christian and the post-Christian.

This is an important point. It would be erroneous to imagine that Christian civilization has been tried and has failed when Christian civilization has rather been attempted and never achieved. Indeed putting it like that may be putting it too strongly. For Christian civilization has been but feebly attempted and by few, if we take the concept "Christian" seriously. It may be better to say that Christian civilization has been recommended but never seriously attempted. The drift of this apparent verbal quibbling is toward establishing that the evident decadence of our civilization is not all that different from what Augustine witnessed, and lamentations over it bewail the failure of an essentially humanistic achievement never effectively interpenetrated by the divine society.

St. Augustine amended the Platonic recipe for the ideal city. Plato laid emphasis on the due relationship of part to part, function to function, station to station, in the ordering of the ideal society. St. Augustine saw all human relationships as properly sustained only on the basis of the relationships of all men to God. This, of course, is the only possible Christian view of human relationships. They are right not by virtue of some delicately negotiated inter-patterning *per se*; they are right by virtue of the preeminent relationship of all men to God. A simpler way of putting this is to say that there is no such thing as universal brotherhood except within the context of a common fatherhood.

"Remove righteousness, and what are kingdoms but great bands of brigands?" Augustine asks. And for Augustine "righteousness" carries a wholly God-centered connotation. Only on the basis of commonly shared faith in God and obedience to his will can there be healthy relationships at the human level. This, of course, is a basic tenet of Christian ethics. It is an inescapable foundation stone for any theory or practice — psychological, social, educational, personal — claiming the label "Christian." If such theories or practices are not grounded in faith and obedience, they are not specifically Christian. So far so good. We may be judged to have made a debating point which the humanist (and perhaps even the radical theologian) would concede. But of course for St. Augustine, and for us if we are Christians, the matter goes much further than that. For Augustine does not argue that, if you remove "righteousness" (a matter of faith and grace) you will be left with an unChristian civilization, a pagan polity. No, he argues that if you remove "righteousness" (a matter of faith in God and the working out of his grace), you will be left with "bands of brigands" in place of an ordered society.

If St. Augustine is right, then it would seem to follow that without that centripetal turning of all hearts to God, you cannot achieve a justly ordered society. You have to be content with brigandage. It would appear that there is no such thing as a justly ordered society except one interpenetrated by human faith and divine grace.

Now some readers may consider that "bands of brigands" is not a bad description of our modern democratic societies, where power groups entirely devoid of ethical principle sack and pillage the minds and hearts and pockets of their fellows. What are great industrial combines, what are the organs of the press, broadcasting and television, what are the filmmakers and presenters, the advertisers, the credit financiers, the corruptors of youth whether in school or out of school, but bands of brigands? St. Augustine has an apt little parable describing an encounter between a captured pirate and his captor, Alexander of Macedon. "How dare you molest the seas?" the pirate was asked. "How dare you molest the whole world?" he countered. "I do it with a little ship and I'm called a thief. You do it with a great navy and you're called an emperor."

"How dare you corrupt a young child?" asks the law today of the arrested pervert. "And how dare you corrupt an entire generation?"

he might ask in reply of the national establishment that condemns him. "I do it on a small scale in my bedroom and it's called criminality. You do it with all the machinery of film, television, press, advertisement, and schools, battering at a million hearts and homes, and it's called Communication or Education." We might twist the parable a little further. "How dare you try to force money from a man by threatening to betray his guilty secret to the world?" the law asks of the convicted blackmailer. And the guilty man might well counter by turning upon the leaders of his country's unions. "How dare you try to force money from millions of fellow countrymen by threatening to deprive innocent citizens of fuel? I do it on a small scale and it's called blackmail. You do it on a national scale and it's called industrial action."

Evil acts, like those of perversion or blackmail, do not become virtuous acts by being practiced on the institutional instead of on the individual level. There seems to be an assumption abroad in our Western democracies that if enough people support a given act then that support confers virtue on the act. Thus individual leverage exercised for selfish ends is rightly seen as wicked and greedy, while mass leverage exercised for selfish ends is viewed as healthily democratic. There is a crude illogicality to be corrected. Corrupting the young does not cease to be corruption just because millions of votes corroborate the practice. We are in danger of giving the voting system the same role in our modern mythology as the philosopher's stone had in ancient superstition. "This is the famous stone / That turneth all to gold." Pronounce a decision democratically arrived at and you have automatically pronounced it "right" and "good."

There is no such magic about mass approval even when expressed through the ballot box. For righteousness cannot always be guaranteed to top the poll. Yet as Christians we know that St. Augustine is right, that without righteousness human society is reduced to brigandage. And righteousness lives only where man has faith in God and God's grace works in man. That is righteousness by definition. And we have plenty of evidence now that a godless society is a system of tolerated brigandage. Secularism is bankrupt. The fact that, as has been said already, there is widespread secular disillusionment with secularism alongside the inevitable Christian distrust of secularism, bears testimony to the bankruptcy. We have

noted the ironic absurdity in the spectacle of so-called Christian
theologians trying to adjust religious thinking to accommodate the
criteria of a secularism discredited even among secularists. The
bolstering of the sagging secular self-confidence by wayward Christians would be farcical if it were not tragic; for, after all, the
puncturing of secular self-confidence is itself a prelude to faith. The
Prince of this World is judged, and it ill becomes Christian theologians to appeal for his reprieve and plan his re-enthronement. Here
is no abiding city, and it is inappropriate therefore for Christian
theologians to try to modify the claims of the eternal kingdom of
God to suit its ephemeral fashions and fancies. "In the world ye
shall have tribulation: but be of good cheer; I have overcome the
world." Our good cheer, be it noted, is based on the fact that the
world has been overcome; it is based on the fact that, whatever
happens, God rules. It is not based on any false confidence in the
earthly setup. The Christian looks at the human scene knowing
that man is a fallen being. He is aware of original sin, the bias of
nature which allows pride and selfishness to corrupt good intentions, and evil to penetrate and permeate the social institutions
devised by man. That is why the Christian is not bowled over by
great national scandals like Watergate. He is distressed, but not
astonished. He always knew that we are all miserable sinners. The
Christian's confidence is not undermined by revelations of corruption in high places, for his confidence never rested in man's own
righteousness but in God's.

The Christian is not surprised either that selfish exploitation of
the earth's resources leads to miles of beaches fouled by oil, sea
birds poisoned and marine life defiled. He is not surprised because
he knows it is the nature of selfishness to produce havoc and deso-
lation. Some of our leaders talk as though it were possible by
means of the corporate state, that is by means of cunningly organized selfishness, to produce harmony and prosperity all round.
Well, our cunningly organized selfishness in the matter of world
transport has given us our defiled beaches and dead sea birds. What
of the fishermen bereft of their livelihoods overnight as by the flick
of a demonic wand? When our Lord dealt with the disheartened
fishermen who had toiled all night and caught nothing, he told
them to launch out on the deep, and they returned with laden nets.

But then there were no oil slicks on the Sea of Galilee. What would he have done if there had been? Perhaps we can conjecture from a study of his characteristic responses. We know his way of dealing with straight human need from the stories of the great catch of fish and the feeding of the five thousand. But when it came to dealing with defilement his approach was different. We know that from the way he drove the money-changers from the temple. Defilement called for a knotted rope.

The Christian's expectation that human affairs will go awry if God is left out of things has nothing in common with the pessimism of the nihilistic dramatist who reduces the human scene to farcical absurdity. The Christian's realism about the world is rooted in his sense of divine Providence. Indeed the Christian's stance in relation to the changes and chances, the follies and wickednesses of this fleeting world is something of a balancing act. On the one side is his trust of God's goodness; on the other side his distrust of man's unaided capacities. In short, his stance is determined by the doctrine of Providence and the doctrine of Original Sin.

The doctrine of divine Providence teaches us to lay all matters before God in sorrow or joy, worry or hope. When we tussle therefore with a testing personal problem like disease or bereavement, we know it is our Christian duty to ask God to see us through and to make the experience fruitful. When we tussle with political problems, social problems, or intellectual problems, it is obviously our duty to do the same. We must not assume that God loses interest when we turn to political, social or educational matters. We are not dealing with an apathetic or illiterate God of whom it must be assumed that anything other than the most strictly intimate matters of personal well-being and personal relationships are outside his competence. But granting that, it is not enough to imagine that a few slogans about "Christian relevance" will get us very far—or to assume that an infusion of untutored Christian idealism in the shape of naive radicalism salted with sentimentality is going to help anyone grapple with grave social and economic problems on a world scale.

The word "relevance" ought to be examined in this connection, for it can be argued that the familiar slogans about Christianity being relevant to this and that underplay rather than overstate the

Christian demand. If someone told you that a supply of gasoline was relevant to the smooth running of your car, you would suspect him of making a feeble joke, for of course gasoline is essential to the smooth running (or even the rough running) of your car. If someone told me that a supply of writing paper was relevant to the completion of this book and the production of a satisfactory manuscript, I should similarly question the use of the word "relevant," not because it put the matter too strongly but because it represented an absurd understatement. Writing paper is essential to the production of my manuscript. St. Augustine for one is not saying that righteousness (by which he means the operation of man's faith and God's grace) is relevant to the proper functioning of society; he is saying that it is essential to the maintenance of truly human relationships within that society — so essential that to take it away is to replace ordered polity by competitive brigandage.

It might be helpful to seek an analogy at the human level. You would not describe learning parts and rehearsing as relevant to the production of a play. Learning and rehearsing may not be as essential to the performance of a play as gas is to the running of a car or paper to the making of a book, for there would be no movement of the car without gas and no book to read without paper; while, on the other hand, it is conceivable that something called a "performance" of a play could be put on by actors who had neither learned their parts nor rehearsed together. But it would be a very bad performance indeed. Something would be happening; superficially what happened would have the outer marks of a performance of the play in question; actors would be moving about the stage, mouthing sentences and perhaps pushing the simulated story vaguely in the direction in which it was supposed to go. But if it were supposed to be *Pygmalion* then Bernard Shaw would turn in his grave. Moreover legal action might be possible against the players for misrepresenting to the public what they were supposed to be about.

This is a convenient analogy for purposes of the present argument. It is possible to fashion a system of public life, an apparently ordered society, without the Christian righteousness declared by Augustine to be essential; but the resulting human performance would be on a par with the stage performance of the unlearned, unrehearsed play. On the stage you would see a travesty of *Pygmalion*. On the stage of life you see a travesty of what a civilized society should be. And oddly enough, at the end of this little metaphorical excursion, we reach a conclusion that many intelligent people, and not necessarily Christians, would accept as valid. Our national communities are indeed travesties of what civilized societies should be.

If you say only that rehearsing is relevant to dramatic production you imply that drama can manage without it, perhaps at a pinch. If you say only that Christianity is relevant to the life of an ordered society, you imply that an ordered society can manage without it. It all depends what you mean by "manage." You can put your performance on the stage of the theater or on the stage of life without a discipline of rehearsal in the one case, without the discipline of Christian righteousness in the other case; but in either case your performance will be a travesty of the real thing.

The reader should now take note where our argument (piloted by St. Augustine) has led us. We began by surmising that civilization is a prerequisite of Christianity; we end by concluding that Christianity is a prerequisite of true civilization. The contradiction is apparent only.

For purposes of argument, we have spoken as though secular society stood over against Christianity in total opposition. But our Western societies do not by any means wholly lack "righteousness" in the Augustinian sense, for they contain very large numbers of Christians who have faith in God and allow his grace to work in them and through them. Thus the parallel of the unlearned lines and the unrehearsed play whose performance is a travesty of the real thing is a theoretical hypothesis only. We are all on the stage. Some of us, being Christians, have tried to learn our lines and have got together for disciplined rehearsal in the great drama of life. So *Pygmalion* will not after all be a total shambles. There will, here and there, be well-rehearsed sections, well-conned exchanges of dialogue. Some actors know their parts and are under instruction from that Director to whom all would be submitting in obedience were everything happening in accordance with his great design.

One hesitates to push the analogy even to this point. It seems to imply that Christians are the only people who are up to any good in life at all and that everyone else is contributing to a general chaos. Of course it is not so simple as that. All parables oversimplify for the purpose of making their point. Our parable here is intended primarily to shift the reader's angle of vision, to show the inadequacy of thinking in terms of a Christian Church *here* and a secular society *there*, and more particularly of then discussing the *relevance* of the one to the other. The very word *relevance* implies relationship between two distinct but possibly relatable forms or bodies. There is no such distinction between the Christian Church and secular society. The two interpenetrate one another. Wherever the Church is at work in society, society at that point ceases to be "secular." Secularism is isolation from Christianity. Each of us, if he practices his Christianity seriously, transforms society at the point of that practice into a religious, a Christian society. The Christianizing of society is precisely such a matter of inner penetration. It is convenient in verbal usage to distinguish between secular activities like mending a burst pipe and religious activities like going to church and praying. But the Christian plumber does not transform himself from a believer into an unbeliever when he rises from his knees and picks up a tool bag to get back to the job. The infusion of Christianity into the human situation that occurs when a prayerful God-fearing man arrives at your door to fix a burst pipe is clearly not definable in the same way as the infusion of Christianity into the human situation when a schoolteacher who is a devout evangelist takes over the class of which your child is a member. This distinction is one that we shall have to develop later; nevertheless personal contacts, however fleeting, are never quite the same when the Christian touch is upon them.

However, it is more important to note that the converse is also true. Just as penetration by Christian thinking and doing transforms secular society at the point of impact into a Christian society (the secular being only that area of life which is untouched by religion, and an area therefore that we Christians have power to diminish and whittle away by our Christian commitment and articulation), so, in the same way, penetration by secular thinking and doing transforms a religious body at the point of impact into a purely secular society. Thus, as Christians have power to intrapenetrate secular society and Christianize it, so secularists have

power to intrapenetrate Christian society, the Church, and secular-
ize it. Now it will be evident that this is precisely what has been
happening to the Church in many cases during the past two decades. People wholly imbrued with the secularist outlook, who
make all their judgments by reference to secular criteria, have intrapenetrated our ministries, our theological seminaries, and our
organs of supposed "Christian" publicity. They have propagated
teachings which imply that the Christian's duty in society is not to
transform by that infusion of faith which opens up the channels of
grace and thus redirects all activities by the compass of Augustinian
"righteousness," but to lubricate the machinery of secular activity
with the oil of humanistic altruism and to stoke up the clamor of
self-assertiveness and possessiveness among the deprived and
underprivileged. It is ironic that the "underprivileged" are sometimes definable by reference to deficiency of those possessions
which people of sagacity and integrity have foresworn in their
pursuit of peace.

In so far as the Church is infiltrated by the secular ethos, it is
intrapenetrated by evil. Because the agents of infiltration are often
themselves ministers and "theologians," simple people are bemused
into acquiescence with policies and activities with which their
deeper Christian sensitivities are ill at ease. The process of corrupting the laity is made easier today by the evident necessity to live in
peace, tolerance, and friendliness with people of other faiths. But
any attempt—upon the basis of this civil necessity—to turn the
multi-faith society into a "good thing" *per se* (and therefore more
"Christian" in its jolly all-in-the-same-boat multiplicity than a truly
Christian society would be!) is plainly diabolical in origin. The
Church's duty to people of other faiths is to convert them, nothing
less. A "Christianity" which has lost the impetus to do so has turned
its back on the primary message of the New Testament. The
attempt to give a "Christian" blessing to the multi-faith society as
such is wholly secularist in purpose.

Existing harmoniously and charitably alongside people of other
faiths and people of no faith at all is a matter of basic decency. It is
a virtue in our national societies that they do what they can by
legislation to encourage the peaceful and mutually respectful co-

existence of men and women thus separated by creed. This proper principle of toleration may engender a sense of national together- ness across the boundaries of belief that bears fruit in healthy public endeavor. The Christian does not decry such communal im- pulses when he asserts that they provide no basis or excuse for overlooking or soft-pedalling the claim that only in Christ is salvation to be found.

"Two loves have created two cities; love of self, to the contempt of God, the earthly city; love of God to the contempt of self, the heavenly city," St. Augustine wrote. Now it is true that we must not identify our national society as the earthly city and the Church as the heavenly city. St. Augustine did not. The two cities exist in antithesis, and our nations and churches are not so related in oppo- sition. Far from it. The two interpenetrate each other. And in so far as the nation serves ends other than the love of self, it is something more wholesome and worthy than Augustine's "earthly city." Similarly, in so far as the Church serves ends other than the love of God, and what naturally follows from it in the way of human duty, it is to that extent less wholesome than St. Augustine's "heavenly city." The heavenly city is an ideal, and the Church is an institution operative in a faulty and often hostile world. But it is only by reference to the values and criteria of that ideal city that the Chris- tian can find his proper footing in the contemporary world.

We have seen current secular civilization under judgment by Christians and by secularists themselves; we have heard the ques- tion aired whether our educational and our cultural development may not have gone into reverse; and we have noted the charge that authority and reason are being superseded by anti-authority and unreason. The current civilizational turning-point represented by these developments has been seen in parallel with that which confronted St. Augustine when the fall of Rome impelled him to the composition of *De Civitate Dei*, and he prescribed Christian righteousness as the only alternative to general brigandage. The essential interdependence of Christianity and just civilization is the Augustinian principle. The complex interpenetration of Christian Church and godless secularism is the reality that confronts us.

2

Where do we stand against secularism?

THE INTERPENETRATION OF the Christian Church and secular society challenges Christians to be alertly sensitive to the characteristics of the Christian faith which distinguish Christians from others with whom their aims overlap in wanting to live good lives and make a better world. The reason for saying this must not be misunderstood. At the practical level, in an emergency, when two men, the one a Christian, the other an atheist, rush together to rescue a motorist trapped in a burning car, questions of faith are not ostensibly at issue. Saving the man is a matter of presence of mind, resourcefulness in laying hands on a fire extinguisher or a hammer, and of course courage. We will not go into the question whether the fact that the Christian, by habit, mutters a prayer, makes a difference to the observable outcome. Christian judgments and evaluations are so entangled with issues of well-being transcending those of physical survival that the measurement of such chances becomes irrelevant.

Nevertheless, in the matter of good works — at least of improving the physical and material lot of fellow men — there is an area of achievement in which rough measurements of progress can be made, and our age has certainly seen considerable social progress in many areas of human welfare. Christians have played their part in this progress. Those of us who were young during the inter-war years are not tempted to underestimate the importance of Christian movements for social justice. We remember seeing hungry children on slum streets with bare feet and torn clothing. We remember seeing weary, unkempt, jobless men (the heroes of the Western Front) lounging dejectedly at streetcorners or knocking cringingly on the back door and pleading to sell you something from a miserable cardboard tray of darning wool, elastic, tape, and string, whose total negotiable value would scarcely have purchased a single square meal. If we who were at that time brought up as Christians believed anything with fervor, it was that in the name of Christ the social order that produced such humiliations and injustice must be transformed root and branch. It is necessary to say this with maximum force and emphasis lest the drift of this book be misunderstood and — whether misunderstood or not — misrepresented.

Having said it, we note that Christians were not the only people to be stirred by this sense of social outrage. They were not alone in striving for the social and political changes which have at least mitigated these particular horrors in our own Western countries even if they have left many comparable injustices still to be tackled both at home and abroad. Having admitted that we Christians neither were nor are alone in our zeal for social justice, we logically imply that a concern for social justice is not a characteristic which preeminently distinguishes a Christian from a non-Christian. The paradox is that there is both a great deal of difference and (in another sense) no effective difference at all between the impulse which says, "This system must be changed" and the impulse which says, "In the name of Christ this system must be changed."

The fact that we share with non-Christians certain aims relative to the amelioration of the material conditions in which fellow human beings live is certainly not to be regretted. It is to be wel-

comed. But, in welcoming it, we must not forget that we have arrived at a common junction on our way to very different destina-
tions and motivated by very different purposes. Indeed at such
points of overlap with humanistic endeavors there may be a special
need to make some noise about the fact that an overlap is not an
identification. We share certain practical aims with non-Christians.
Precisely because we share them, we must beware lest our message
to the world seems to consist in nothing more than this shared program. Christian preaching and teaching must take account of this
problem. Otherwise, exhortation may fasten exclusively on those
aspects of Christian teaching which are not peculiar to Christianity.
The recommendation to work for social and economic justice in undeveloped countries and to minister at home to the sick, the needy,
the aged, and the distressed, is an indispensibly important part of
the Christian message. Yet a non-Christian could justly object if
Christians seemed to be claiming a monopoly or exclusive proprietorship in fields of social amelioration and general beneficence.
Moreover non-Christians may well begin to suspect that we are
ashamed of the unshared, the specifically and exclusively *Christian*
aspects of our faith and practice, if we play them down persistently
in favor of programs and purposes that men of decency and good-
will share across the boundaries of faith and creed.

Healthy Christian thought and teaching are often a matter of
delicate balance between mutually opposed emphases. Paradox is
threaded through our Christian way of thinking. Christianity is
concerned with all aspects of life, but the Christian can be so busy
being concerned that he forgets to be a Christian. Perhaps the point
can be illustrated by analogy. Imagine a TV program in which a
number of tradesmen are interviewed in order to elicit their various
angles on trade. The team includes a butcher, a grocer, a bookseller, and a milliner. The butcher takes the lead and talks about
problems of interest and taxes, overheads and profit margins, the
employment of assistants, the insurance of property, and so on.
Now all these are important matters to him, but in fact they are
problems shared equally with the grocer, the bookseller, and the
milliner. So he is really speaking as a shopkeeper, not specifically as
a butcher. If he is going to give the butcher's angle, then he will
have to talk about meat, because the *differentia* of the butcher (the

thing that makes the butcher different from the others) is that he deals in meat. *Differentiae* is an ugly word, but it means precisely those attributes of a thing which make it different.

It may be argued that Christian exhortation has become disproportionately concerned with the characteristics of Christianity which, though important, are not *differentiae*, not the things that make it different. This slant in presentation can easily be misleading to non-Christians, disquieting to Christians, and confusing to both. It is a matter of emphasis. We are obviously not saying that the butcher is any the less an honest butcher when he talks about taxes than when he talks about meat, still less that he is necessarily any less interesting. He will be a bore if he never talks about anything but meat.

We must not press the analogy too far. No doubt there are still pulpits from which the *differentiae* of Christianity are rigorously pressed home while all-important characteristics shared between Christians and humanists are neglected or ignored; and this will not do. If we do not want a Christian sermon to be indistinguishable from a humanist appeal for Oxfam, neither do we want the Sacrifice of the Mass to be the beginning, middle, and end of every sermon. And we do not want the call to personal salvation in Jesus Christ to be the center, area, and circumference of every sermon. Certainly this is material of exclusively Christian teaching *per se*; but it can be the heart and core of comprehensive exhortation — spiritual, moral, practical, and social — only if the heart is not mistaken for the whole body, the core for the whole apple.

At present we seem in some quarters more likely to neglect the heart and core than to over-emphasize them. We need to remember that many of those personal virtues and private good deeds which we call practical Christianity someone else may cultivate and call them practical humanism. And those ventures in social amelioration which we recommend as applied Christianity someone else may undertake and call them applied socialism. The heart and core, the motive and origin of our application lie in facts of Christian revelation and Christian commitment that the humanist does not share. But that is not self-evident to all and sundry. So there are two alternative mistakes to be avoided. At the opposite extreme to the "Sacrifice of the Mass" sermon and the "Salvation in Christ" sermon which hardly overstep the boundaries of personal spiritual pietism are the "Third World" sermon and the "Caring for Others" sermon which may be moving, noble, and compassionate, and yet scarcely say anything that a virtuous humanist would not concur in.

The problem is not confined to the pulpit. One has listened to discussions broadcast or televised in which more or less eminent people have addressed themselves publicly to problems of the day — perhaps a politician, a scientist, a writer, and a bishop. And the chairman said to the bishop: "Perhaps you could give us the Christian angle on this problem." The bishop obliged, speaking with concern, understanding, and compassion, speaking indeed like a virtuous man. But so did the others. They all spoke like virtuous and compassionate men. Where was the difference? In what did the Christian angle consist? Are there Christians who no longer claim to be anything other than people of humane altruism? Is this what acting and speaking as a Christian has come to mean? Has it no longer anything to do with bringing to bear upon human issues the great facts of revelation and redemption in Christ? What about being filled with the Holy Spirit, rejoicing in the good news of the Resurrection, and carrying it to the furthest corners of the earth? Are not these essential priorities of Christian witness and proclamation?

Christianity has no monopoly of helping, healing, and caring, but it has its own unique doctrines of redemption and salvation in Christ summed up in creed and sacrament. Do not mistake my purpose in stressing this. It is not to assert pietism at the expense of social service or even faith at the expense of works. It is not to suggest that we spend too much time in acts of ministry to others. Most of us spend far too little time thus. But there is need for a clear-minded distinction which could help us in the future to be more effective witnesses and evangelists. This needed distinction can be pin-pointed in two questions and the answers they respectively call for: (1) What should I, as a good man or woman, do or say in this case? and (2) What should I, as a Christian, do or say in this case? The Christian ought always to be a good man or woman, and therefore the answer to 1 will be contained in the answer to 2. But there will be things in the answer to 2 which are not contained

in the answer to 1, and they are the things which today we are inclined to neglect.

There are notable reasons for suggesting that we may have
passed through the phase when the pressing question was: What
makes Christianity relevant? to a phase when the most urgent question is: What makes Christianity different? What are the characteristics of the Christian faith which distinguish Christians from others
who want to live good lives and make a better world?

The reasons for this change lie in the character of our culture. In
many respects our Christian commitment puts us on a collision
course with contemporary culture — as has already been
evidenced — but not in all respects, perhaps not even in most
respects. And because there are areas of action where Christian endeavor joins forces with important currents of secular endeavor,
the need for the kind of disentanglement that this book attempts is
important, perhaps urgent.

The antithesis between the Church and the World is essential to
Christian thinking. Nothing has been more damaging to the Christian cause during the last fifteen or twenty years than the assumption by some Christians that there is something outmoded in the
notion of conflict between the Church and the World. We accept,
of course, that the expression "the World" is used in a variety of
ways. However, the Biblical connotation which opposes the Christian to the World is a necessary device for defining the Christian's
otherworldly affiliation to an order whose criteria of love, obedience, and self-sacrifice are antithetic to everything we mean by
worldliness. Yet a habit has grown up in some circles in recent
years of rightly asserting that this is God's world, and then subtly
insinuating that the Biblical antithesis between the Church and the
World is therefore obsolete. We have been treated to emphases
upon the Incarnation which covertly carry the innuendo that anyone who finds anything wrong with a world which God himself
entered and a human nature which God himself embraced is thereby blaspheming divine creation. One has heard anarchistic
utterances — overturning morality, rationality, and even ordinary
human decency — assuming a pseudo-sacred veneer by this mis-
chievous misrepresentation. The Incarnation was, after all, the

basis of a rescue operation for fallen man. It is not the prior fact of the Christian revelation. The Creation comes first. When God entered the world in human form, he came to a fallen world with the purpose of offering redemption from sin; it ill becomes us to pretend that we have no sins to be redeemed from. Had God's incarnation in Christ itself obliterated sin from the human scene and restored man to his pristine innocence, then there would have been no need of a Crucifixion.

The clash between the Church and the World must not be underplayed, but it is not the same thing as the collision between Christianity and contemporary culture. The two oppositions must be differentiated. The clash between the Church and the World is basic and clear-cut. It is the clash between service to Christ and service to the Prince of this World, between everything that calls us to set our hearts on things above and everything that lures us to make physical well-being in this world the be-all and end-all. The collision between Christianity and contemporary culture is neither so basic nor so clear-cut; indeed, it will vary in character and intensity from age to age and from country to country. It is obviously not the same, for instance, in the Soviet Union and in the United States. The collision will be more or less violent in so far as the culture in question is either hostile to the Church's teaching and practice or tolerant of and friendly to that teaching and practice. The word "culture" is being used here in a general sense — the civilizational setup in which we are all caught up.

There are certain respects in which our contemporary Western culture is more in tune with Christian ideals than perhaps any previous culture. One may mention our concern for the poor, the sick, and the afflicted; the safeguards we provide for them at home, and the attempts we make to alleviate suffering abroad. The Third World is on our conscience whether we are Christians or not. Contemporary culture as we know it in our countries will not tolerate the cruelties of child-labor and the virtual or actual slavery on which some of our nineteenth-century industries depended. Contemporary opinion is against exploitation of the underprivileged. In these ways contemporary culture is less "worldly" than it was a century ago when it was perhaps more officially "Christian." On the other hand, we cannot pretend that at the intellectual level contemporary culture is more in tune today with Christian understanding of man's nature and destiny than it was a century ago.

The change which has brought certain currents of thought and action in contemporary culture more into line with what the Christian conscience can welcome and support has produced its problems as well as its great blessings. It is important to recognize what these problems are, especially at a time when the Church is giving so much of its attention to the social gospel. For Christians, it can be a stimulating business nowadays to come to grips with specific social corruptions precisely because the assault upon injustice, cruelty, and poverty carries with it the public support of leading elements in our secular civilization. But the fact that it is respectable and fashionable nowadays to be socially conscious does not prove it the most urgent priority of Christian witness. It may by contrast be a forbidding task to turn from the social to the intellectual front, and to attack established modes of thought which have the backing of contemporary academic circles with their vast intellectual authority and influence; but the formidableness of the challenge ought surely not to deflect us from taking it up. Indeed the formidableness of the challenge is the measure of its importance. If the change in the temper of our culture is such that we Christians can enjoy being in the vanguard of social progress in the struggles against material injustice, it is also such that we are tempted to shrink from the mental fight, for the prospect of espousing causes which the established and fashionable intellectual circles of our time tend to regard as obscurantist and fanciful is neither attractive nor invigorating. In short, the twentieth-century Christian social gospel for the world in its practical manifestations is now in tune with powerful currents of thought outside the Church; but the Christian's unchanging understanding of man's nature and vocation is at loggerheads with established thinking. Is it not therefore incumbent upon us to adjust our priorities, and to strive to counter intellectual apostasy with the same buoyancy and relish with which we confront social injustice?

The social gospel focuses attention so sharply on earthly well-being that we naturally find ourselves in alliance with secular trends as we try to put it into practice; and this alliance carries with

it the danger of blanketing the basic *differentiae* of Christian commitment. The Christian social gospel may be desperately needed
and yet not be the overriding need at a time when our culture is
under attack from the forces of disintegration and nihilism. It
would be naive to assume that if the Christian social gospel is
preached, the gospel of redemption will take care of itself; indeed,
it would be quite improper to tackle social problems with an eye on
some calculated spin-off in the form of queues for baptism. The
caricature of the Victorian do-gooder tendering a bowl of soup
with one hand and a Bible with the other is not a fit model. But the
very absurdity of treating Christian conversion as a by-product of
fruitful social welfare work underlines the converse point that
social welfare work is in fact an inevitable by-product of Christian
conversion. Wherever the gospel of the resurrection has been
preached and heard, hospitals have been built and the poor fed.
The logical priority of the gospel of redemption is unquestionable.

There is no intention here to belittle the efforts of Christians who
in difficult circumstances, under unjust and tyrannical governments, are heroically striving to improve the lot of the poor and the
oppressed. Rather the argument is directed to the minds and wills
of those Christians whose work lies in free and affluent environ-
ments like our own, where choosing between the social gospel and
the re-integration of the Christian mind may be more a matter of
selecting a subject for a sermon or a study group than of more practical action.

Our present absorption with the social gospel rather than with
the Christian mind determines the character of our Christian dilemma. It was not always so. One does not need to be a very knowl-
edgeable student of history to realize that in these respects the
situation of the medieval Christian would have been the very reverse of ours. He would be in tune with the dominant cultural influences of the day when he reasoned for the validity of the Christian synthesis in the world of intellect. And he would be at loggerheads with the contemporary establishment had he in practice
taken up the cause of social equality and emancipation. Our perils
are not the same as our ancestors' were. We are in no danger of establishing an Inquisition, of protecting the purity of dogma by
lopping off people's hands or sending them to the stake. Our risk is

rather that too exclusive a concentration of Christian endeavor in the social field will weaken awareness of the Church as a body rooted in the supernatural. It encourages the notion that Christianity is a kind of sentimental humanitarianism with a top-dressing of decorative religiosity. There are people about today who believe that the essence of Christian mission lies in the dissemination of good fellowship, the ubiquitous cultivation of pleasant and pleasurable personal relationships, the bringing of comfort and aid to the sick and afflicted, and the elimination of tension and discomfort from a multi-national and multi-racial world. All these things are tremendously important. Yet these ends can be served without ever bringing into the arena of thought the basic Christian truths of the divine creation, man's fall, the incarnation and redemption, and the vocation pressing upon all of us to worship a God who loves us, died for us, and calls us to everlasting life. The risk we run is that the reality of the supernatural will become a vague, remote conceptual background against which a supposedly Christian program for personal behavior and social amelioration is worked out.

The truth is that the Christian holds a certain distinctive view of what life is all about, a certain distinctive view of what kind of creatures we are, how we ought to live here and now, and what is in store for us hereafter. In short, there is a Christian doctrine of man; a Christian statement about man's nature, his duties, and his ultimate destiny; and it differs sharply from dominant secularist assumptions.

Yet there are also attributes of Christian theory and practice which are shared by altruistic unbelievers — the idea of the brotherhood of man, for instance, and concern for the material welfare of all people of all races. The emphatic propagation of such ends by Christians carries the danger that our minds will become so attuned to operating alongside unbelievers in the sphere of shared social idealism that the specific Christian motivation of our work will be submerged publicly in silence and privately in sheer busyness. It is an urgent matter that we Christians should find a habitual mode of thinking, speaking, and living which publicly clarifies the character of the Christian message — and indicates its sweeping dynamism, its all-embracing coherence. The words "publicly clarifies" are used advisedly. For there is evidence that the Christian life can be lived by devout and earnest men and women who abound in good works and in private spiritual discipline, and yet the impact they make on their fellowmen will fail for purposes of what (if no better word is available) one might call propaganda. The helpfulness, the compassion, the generosity—all these may come through, and yet the specific "Christianness" of it may fail to be evident. The differentness of the Christian action fails to make itself felt, and it is the differentness that challenges secularist values sharply.

What we need in this respect is a state of mind rather than a set of rules. From time to time in life one comes across wise and experienced Christians who are adept at giving that little twist to a conversation which suddenly casts a new light on the matter at issue by a hint of how it might look in the eyes of heaven. A sentence is said, and suddenly the perspectives of earthly life are transcended. Sometimes the effect is to comfort distress; sometimes to jolt complacency.

But most of us, clergy and laity alike, tend to blunt the edge of Christian thinking and blur the outlines of Christian action by playing down motives grounded in prayer and worship, perspectives derived from the framework of supernatural truth. The expression "play down" does not mean only that we refrain from talking directly about these matters—though indeed it is no doubt true that we do so refrain—but rather that we forget these matters inwardly and, as a result, the contribution we bring to the common thinking excludes the angle or emphasis that might fruitfully illuminate, stir, or even jolt our fellows in a Christian direction. This angle or emphasis need not itself be an overtly religious utterance, a pious reminder. But there are angles and emphases—sometimes subtle and oblique—which are rooted in Christian consciousness, as there are angles and emphases which reflect an unbaptized imagination. And indeed you might get the latter in a religious sermon and you might get the former in an observation which on the surface has no religious flavor.

Two contrasting examples recur to me, interesting for the way they have remained in my memory. The first takes me back nearly fifty years. I was a choirboy, aged about twelve, taking part in an outdoor Sunday afternoon service held in a cricket field and designed to draw a congregation of men—which it did. I seem to re-member a brass band and surplices floating in a light June breeze. The sermon was preached by a parish priest whose forthright, even aggressive, style gave him the reputation of being a man's man; that was why he had been invited for the occasion. One of his sentences has stayed in my mind ever since. He was making a forceful protest against the action of some bereaved parents who had had the words "Thy will be done" inscribed above the grave of their child, a victim of typhoid. "Don't blame God," he shouted. "Blame the Sanitary Inspector!"

Now this sounded fine indeed to a boy of twelve, and perhaps in its full context it did no damage. The preacher was quite right to draw attention, especially at that time (about 1929, I guess) to the need to get on with the job of making a better, more hygienic environment for our fellow-citizens. Yet this sentence, which at first jolted me with delight for its message, gradually began to seem more and more questionable as I grew older. At last it fixed itself in my mind as a specimen of the opposite kind of emphasis from that which the Christian's thinking ought to convey. At least "Thy will be done" hands over the mind and heart to God, at the end of the child's life, in prayerful acceptance. The sentence is itself the key to Christian morality. It is, in T.S. Eliot's words, "the hardly, barely prayable / Prayer of the one Annunciation" under which all annun-ciations are subsumed, all incarnations effected. "Be it unto me according to thy word." Ought Christian preaching ever to take up a statement with Christian dimensions, reject it, and substitute a statement on the level of material causation from which the reli-gious dimension has been obliterated? The experience was long ago; a childhood memory may be unreliable; perhaps this use of his words is unjust to a worthy priest now dead. But the words were said, and they have stayed with me for a lifetime, a symbol of the fact that any Christian stance which downgrades supernatural cri-teria for the purpose of alignment with a popular social cause is open to grave question.

The second example from personal experience also turns on an observation about death that startled me. I was a student at Oxford. One or two of us were discussing some poetry of the First World War with our tutor, C.S. Lewis. He seemed to think we were overestimating the quality of the poetry in question—that it lacked something which it ought to have. "In the whole volume," he said (as nearly as I can remember), "not one of the poets has thought to observe that the dead would have died anyway, war or no war." Whereas the preacher's words quoted above at first jolted me with delight for their message, Lewis' words at this point first jolted me with dismay. There seemed to be a hint of callousness in them (just as there seemed to be a flavor of notable compassion in the assault upon the Sanitary Inspector). But of course Lewis, who had served at the front in the First World War, was the last man to be callous about it, and his books show repeatedly how deeply he admired courage in battle. As I got to know Lewis better, I recognized this statement as the kind of conscious jolt he habitually administered—partly to stimulate his pupils to think about a matter differently and freshly, indeed to save them from cliché-thinking, but also partly because, as a Christian, he could not allow the subject of death to be treated as though termination of life were it itself the ultimate tragedy and a kind of aberration or exception in the human lot. His remark was in no sense a religious statement about death. There was no mention of God or of the life hereafter. Yet it stayed in my memory as a specimen of the kind of contribution which the Christian mind will naturally bring to the common thinking. For it was the product of habitual awareness that there are more important things for us even than our continuing life on this earth, and that our stay here is in all cases a short one anyway.

I have purposely set in opposition a statement which seems to push the mind in the direction of naturalistic, or this-worldly, thinking (though it was made in a sermon and it talked of God) and a statement which seems, however discreetly, to push the mind away from acceptance of the standard naturalistic or this-worldly criteria (though it was made in a tutorial and contained no mention of God) because I feel that we fail time and again to bring our specifically Christian position to bear, even obliquely, upon our contemporaries' thinking.

There are Christian bodies whose practice is to initiate their members by total immersion in baptismal water, and there are people whose minds seem to have been soaked through by "total immersion" in Christian modes of thinking. Lewis was one such.

The fact that he was a man of rare personal spirituality and saintliness and that he also, intellectually, had perhaps the most deeply dyed Christian understanding of our times, raises serious questions. Can the mind attain true Christian insight unless the will is comparably consecrated? Is built-in Christian mental orientation inseparably interconnected with moral obedience? Is knowledge of God acquired only on the further side of commitment? This, and not intellectual inadequacy alone, may be the problem behind aberrant theology in our day.

Our thesis is that the Christian holds a certain view of what life is all about, a certain view of what kind of creatures we are, how we ought to live, and what is in store for us hereafter. There is a Christian doctrine of man; a Christian statement about man's nature, his duties, and his ultimate destiny. This view of life and this doctrine differ sharply from secularist assumptions. The Christian whose mind is baptized by total immersion will have an outlook and a conversation colored by the Christian view of life; but that does not of course mean that he will be forever talking about God. There will be times, no doubt, when it is proper for him to carry on a conversation with a non-Christian in total unanimity of understanding and without any impingement of specifically Christian concepts. This would be the case if he were engaged in a testing game of chess and in postmortem analysis of the game. Can we prescribe at what points in our daily course the difference between ourselves and our non-Christian fellows becomes a pressing one? In how many areas is the specifically Christian doctrine of man a matter of direct concern? The question is asked because it seems that we have slid unthinkingly into the assumption that our Christianity is largely a private and social, not a professional or intellectual matter; that it is a matter of personal morality and social conscience, of cultivating the moral virtues and helping the needy.

It is plain that the Christian doctrine of man, which scarcely has much bearing on our game of chess, likewise has little outward bearing on the activities in which many of us are professionally engaged. If you are employed, say, as a plumber, and you are a Christian, then being a Christian affects your plumbing only in the sense that you try to work honestly and conscientiously and do your best work with a good grace. Being a Christian is not going to alter the rules of good plumbing for you and make them different. There is no such thing as Christian plumbing. No doubt the dedicated man of faith would apply the rules of his craft in a different mood and spirit if he were fitting new wash-basins into a hospital than if he were required to install new heating-pipes in a casino; but this difference of mood or spirit would not be reflected in any difference in workmanship. In other words, questions of ultimate purpose and of moral value may intrude upon us in our performance of technical functions, giving a special human dimension to our attitude, but without affecting the character and quality of the work itself. In the same way considerations of a personal kind impinge upon an individual's daily work by virtue of the fact that no man is just a plumber; he is also a husband, a father, a son, a brother, and in these capacities his daily work bears the stamp of human responsibilities dear to his heart and inseparably connected with whatever religious faith he has. Earning money in due measure itself bears the symbolic weight of personal service to one's family. Rarely is a paycheck merely a ticket to a series of private satisfactions. It is a means of answering the needs of others within the family and without, and on this purpose a man's Christian commitment has a direct bearing.

I am trying to locate the point at which work may assume an overtly Christian character that marks off the performance or product as objectively different in itself quite apart from differences of motivation and attitude in the doer of the work. If you wanted to install a new radiator in a church you would not think it crucial to employ a Christian plumber; but if you wanted a new hymn you would seek around for a Christian poet to write the verses. In the one case Christian commitment is apparently irrelevant to the character and quality of the product itself; in the other case Christian commitment is crucial to the character and quality of the product itself. How do we draw the line between activities of the former and the latter kind? We have failed to think this issue through. We have failed by evasion. The evasion has been made possible by two emphases in our thinking which have kept our minds preoccupied. The first emphasis is the very proper insistence that all the believer's activities should have an implicit Christian orientation, in that everything should be done to the glory of God and out of deep Christian commitment to the service of his fellow men. This principle rightly bypasses the question whether, motive apart, a given activity or its product will *in itself* have a greater or a less, a positive or a negative "Christian" character. The second emphasis is that produced by the fashionable bias which tends to equate "Christian" behavior with "caring and compassionate" behavior. If we are obsessed with the notion that acting "as a Christian" means doing a job conscientiously and caringly, we can easily forget that acting "as a Christian" may sometimes mean doing a different job rather than doing the same job with a different attitude.

Perhaps we use the word "Christian" too glibly anyway, especially as an adjective. Usage is more straightforward so long as the word is a noun. "He is a Christian" has a definite meaning able to be checked by reference to the dictionary. But "Christian" as an adjective is a different matter. ("Christian" was a noun first, and sometimes one is tempted to think that it would have been better had it remained only a noun.) As long as the adjective is used with its full force in expressions like "the Christian Church," "the Christian faith," "Christian baptism" and so on, we know where we are. The same applies to such sentences as "St. Augustine was a great Christian teacher," which clearly means that he was a great exponent of the Christian faith. Yet the expression "Christian teacher" might be used with a very different connotation from this. It appears in obituaries and testimonials applied to people who never taught the faith personally, but who taught chemistry or mathematics on weekdays and went to church on Sundays. One has seen advertisements for "Christian teachers" which appeared to mean simply that respectable men and women without chips on their shoulders were being sought to teach English and Arithmetic in undeveloped countries. There was a time too when genteel ladies would advertise in the press for a "Christian companion" or a "Christian nursemaid," and it was generally assumed that anyone who advertised thus wanted domestic assistance on the cheap. "Christian" became synonymous with "ill-paid."

There is a serious point here. Loose use of the word "Christian" has bedevilled our thinking. We easily lapse into the habit of using it, not as a term of description, but as a term of approval, and for the purpose of the present enquiry it is necessary to clear the ground of ambiguities. When a carpenter who is a Christian makes a door, it may be a good door or a bad door, but it will not be a "Christian" door, even if it is to be used in a church. Yet when a poet writes a poem, not only may it be a good poem or a bad poem, it may also be a Christian poem, an "aChristian" poem, a non-Christian poem (Buddhist perhaps), or even an anti-Christian poem. It may, like one of Donne's "Holy Sonnets," speak of the human lot in terms fully meaningful and acceptable only to the instructed Christian reader. It may, like Wordsworth's "Daffodils," appeal wholly to thoughts and feelings common to people of widely different creeds, or it may, like the verses of Omar Khayyam or like some of Housman's lyrics, express trains of thought antithetical to Christian conviction. And a poem is not necessarily better *as a poem* for being a "Christian" poem in this sense. You can have a bad Christian poem and a good non-Christian poem, as well as vice versa. So "Christian" is certainly not synonymous with "good" in the aesthetic field; nor is it indeed in the moral field. It is highly inaccurate — and grossly unfair to non-Christians — to use "Christian" as a variant of "good" or "virtuous." I do not remember which theologian it was who said, "I will defend to the end the inalienable right of the Christian to be a bad man," but he made a shrewd semantic point. No doubt he expressed it provocatively and in a way likely to cause misunderstanding; but one can sympathize with his determination to employ shock tactics to make clear that the word "Christian" ought never to be used as a mere synonym for "charitable" or "upright" or any other commendatory adjective.

We have established that there are some occupations, like writing poetry, where the finished product might appropriately bring the adjective "Christian" into play, and other occupations, like plumbing, where the finished product could not *in itself* be defined as either "Christian" or "non-Christian," even though it might be designed for use in a church. Even the altar or holy table is not essentially and necessarily differentiable from a table designed for wholly secular use. You might take a refectory table and consecrate it for use in the sanctuary without impropriety. Because poetry differs from carpentry in this respect, it would appear to follow that a poet who was converted to Christianity would find a new kind of demand upon him in respect of the work he did as well as a new demand upon him in his personal moral life. And this particular demand would not apply to the converted carpenter or the converted postman. They would share the converted poet's need to review their personal lives and even their attitudes to their work, but would not find the same need to review their occupational duties in substance. The carpenter would not think it his duty to carve Christian symbols on dining room tables; the postman would not start delivering religious tracts through the mail box in addition to the usual income tax forms.

Modern civilization is highly departmentalized, and perhaps most of us do the kind of work which, for purpose of this argument, is roughly parallel to the carpenter's or the postman's. Becoming a Christian will transform our personal life, but its effect is not necessarily going to show up outwardly in our work in the case of many, perhaps most, occupations. And this is certainly not a question of the relative importance of one's job or of the degree of skill or brainpower it requires. Some of the most demanding and prestigious techniques, like those of the concert pianist and the heart surgeon, are such that conversion to Christianity would rightly not affect them one way or another. We are all more interested in whether our dentist is a skilled dentist than whether he is a practicing Christian. If you are going to have an operation for appendicitis, it will bring no special comfort to you to learn that the surgeon who is to operate conducts a regular Bible class. How he handles the scalpel is what matters to you.

This argument must not be pushed too far. Obviously a doctor who becomes a Christian will have to look at certain professional matters afresh. He may have to change his views and practices in the matter of abortion. He may have to take a different attitude to prescribing contraceptive pills for teenagers. But in most areas of his work, being a good doctor is a question of skill, understanding, sympathy, compassion and so on, characteristics which are not peculiar to Christians—though we would hope that Christians are

more likely than others to excel in the humane virtues. It is significant that when we cited two areas of medical activity where the
doctor's attitude might be gravely affected by conversion to Christianity, we cited two activities over which decisions are not strictly
the prerogatives of medical men as such at all — embryonicide and
collusion with young fornicators. Medical training gives one no
right of judgment in such matters.

It is when we come to those occupations in which work preeminently touches the minds of others that the bearing of Christian
commitment upon professional life will be decisive and indeed
public. That is what puts the poet in a different category from the
pianist, the postman, or the surgeon. If a man sets out to influence
the minds of his fellows by any form of non-technical advice, direction, or commentary upon life, then he is involved in work which
cannot possibly be insulated from the influence of his philosophical
position. Statesmen are a case in point; for a man can scarcely
govern others, helping to determine their pattern of life, without
making manifest in his decisions what kind of creatures he believes
he is governing, and what their ultimate destiny is. The same applies to all writers and to all those who work in the communications
media and whose business it is to influence a nation's thought. And
it is a sober reflection that, by the very nature of current corruption, Christians are less likely to seek work — or if they seek it, to be
able to find it — in the media than non-Christians. One might
hazard a guess that the proportion of committed Christians
working in the communications media is lower than in any other
branch of national life. Certainly the tendentious drift of much
media publicity toward the destruction and undermining of faith
would lend color to this supposition.

Perhaps education is the most crucial sphere of influence where
Christian commitment will transform the professional task.
Training others in specific techniques is one thing; forming the
minds of future generations is a very different thing. You may be
content that your family dentist was efficiently trained and not care
whether he has ever heard of God. You will surely be concerned, if
you are a parent, whether the school teachers who guide your
children's thinking are men and women with values and standards

transcending those of mere material welfare, however proficiently they do their job technically speaking. Indeed the more technically expert your dentist is with his drill, the less you will care whether he is a Marxist or a Methodist. But the more expert your children's teacher is as a molder of minds, the *more* you will care what he is overtly or covertly putting into those minds.

We cannot reduce all human processes to techniques. Yet we have grown so accustomed to thinking in terms of techniques that we have begun to conceive of the human being as a compound of person and technician. The first — the person — marries, makes a home, and has children. The second — the technician — earns his living by doing a job. Becoming a Christian bears upon the first role, but has nothing to do with the second role — or so we imagine. Things have become so topsy-turvy that we make a virtue of making appointments to influential and powerful positions without enquiring into candidates' beliefs. Creeds are private matters. The defect with this kind of thinking is that some professional roles are more personal than technical. This is certainly true of education. The man or woman who is engaged in it cannot leave his personal faith behind him at home, because the very substance of education involves questions about the purpose of life, the nature of man, the duty of man, and the destiny of man.

The reason why the Christian cannot leave his faith behind him at home when he involves himself in academic or educational work is that there is no such thing as intellectual neutrality. If you are not studying and teaching on the assumption that there is a life beyond this one, you are studying and teaching on the assumption that there is not. The notion of cultural neutralism is untenable. If you are not studying and teaching on the assumption that man is a divinely created being with a supernatural vocation, you are studying and teaching on the assumption that he is not. Of course the degree of specific relevance to your mental life of Christian presuppositions varies from subject to subject and from one area of study within a subject to another. But all subjects which are directly concerned with questions of human behavior, human motivation, the quality of human life, and human achievement are pursued under the impress of philosophical assumptions which will be either consonant with Christian thinking or hostile to it.

In a series of lectures on "The Aims of Education," delivered at the University of Chicago in 1950, T.S. Eliot said:

> But the moment we ask about the purpose of anything, we may be involving ourselves in asking about the purpose of everything. If we define education, we are led to ask "What is Man?"; and if we define the purpose of education, we are committed to the question "What is Man for?" Every definition of the purpose of education, therefore, implies some concealed or rather implicit philosophy or theology.

The conclusion is self-evident. Then what are the presuppositions with which the Christian approaches questions of human purpose? Surely the Christian is distinguished from the secularist, roughly speaking, by having a double allegiance—to this life which he shares with the secularist and to another life into which his faith admits him. The Christian is born into the life of nature when the midwife delivers him; he is born into the life of supernature when the Church baptizes him. He keeps himself alive and growing in the order of nature by daily food and sleep. He keeps himself alive and growing in the order of supernature by prayer, worship, and other disciplines of the spiritual life.

We live in nature, in time and space, the physical universe, the life of the senses and the brain which other men live even if they are spiritually dead. We live under God by virtue of our membership in the Church, knowing ourselves rooted in a kingdom which is not of this world and will survive when the physical universe has crumbled. That is the rough picture. The orthodox Christian holds these two aspects of the human situation together in balance—a balance which may involve tension. In bringing Christian thinking to bear upon anything, we regard it in its two aspects, in nature and under God. This applies to the simplest and most complex things in life; simple things like daily meals, for instance. The secularist sees food as the product of the earth and of man's labor. The Christian sees it as that and also as the gift of God—and gives thanks accordingly. The secularist sees other men and women as fellow inhabitants of the universe, fellow citizens. The Christian sees other men and women as all this and something more—sons and daughters of a common Father who have received from him the same gift of life, the same offer of salvation. The Christian way of looking at human beings and their doings is always to see them both in nature and under God.

The Christian teacher will apply this double vision both to his pupils and to his subject. He will learn to look at his pupils not only as children of men but as children of God — fellow beings with souls to save. He will learn to look at the subject he teaches not only as part of the fabric of human knowledge, but also as related to those truths of Christian revelation which sum up our knowledge of life and its meaning.

Too long we have assumed that the Christian's business in education is to keep alive specialist instruction in the Bible. The idea that the Christian faith is a "subject" parallel to other subjects can be damaging. The Christian element in education is not just something which you add on top of a whole lot of other things; Divinity or Religious Knowledge added on top of English, History, Geography, French, Mathematics, and Science, just as you might add one extra course to an already substantial meal. You have enjoyed your soup, fish, meat, and dessert; now you add cheese and cookies to round it all off. You have had your English, History, Science, and Mathematics; and now you add Religious Knowledge to top it off neatly.

This cheese-and-cookies notion of the place of Christianity in education produces absurdities. You get the Christian who gives an orthodox lesson on some New Testament teaching in the morning, perhaps about the Prodigal Son or the parable of the Sower, and then in the afternoon he gives a History lesson which suggests in its implications that the only significance of human life lies in the progress of men to universal material prosperity. One has come across earnest fellows who quite sincerely taught in Sunday school on Sunday the need for Christ's redeeming love, and on Monday pursued educational studies on the assumption that the human situation is one of glorious humanistic achievement to which spiritual reality is at best peripheral, at worst irrelevant. One has come across the person who was prepared to talk on Sunday about the need for Grace, but on Monday pursued psychological studies on the assumption that all man needs for personal well-being is to grow like a tree or bound about self-expressively like a deer.

Let us return to the analogy of the educational meal. Christianity as the extra course on top of the other courses will not do because it is indigestible alongside them — unless the other courses are a good deal healthier than they generally are. One has observed school syllabuses in action which are nothing more than recipes for intellectual stomach ache. English, History, Geography, Mathematics, and Religious Knowledge will not go down together if English, History, Geography, and Mathematics are taught with a humanistic, materialistic, or scientistic slant. Or rather, one should say that English, History, Geography, and Mathematics, taught with a humanistic, materialistic, or scientistic slant, will not go down together with Religious Knowledge unless Religious Knowledge is also taught with a humanistic, materialistic, or scientistic slant — that is, unless it is taught in such a way as to cancel itself out. In far too many institutions this is what has happened. Coherence has been achieved by de-Christianizing "Religious Knowledge" so that it has ceased to form a Christian element in the educational diet.

Christianity, if it is taken seriously, can never be merely an extra course on the educational menu. On the other hand, Christianity clearly does not involve you in a totally different educational meal. Christians need their Mathematics and Science as much as anyone. No doubt the best metaphor to define the place of Christianity in the educational diet is the Biblical one. Christianity is the salt that gives a different flavor to everything you eat without altering its essential character, without eliminating any of its distinctiveness, indeed, on the contrary, forcing its true distinctiveness onto the palate.

So far as the Christian and the secularist are concerned, the problem then is not just that the Christian wants to add something to the educational diet that the secularist would exclude. Christians and secularists have fundamentally different views of what education is all about. This is bound to be the case — because education is the nurturing of human beings to fully human living. And the Christian notion of what constitutes *human* living is different from the secularist's. Christianity has its own specific doctrine of what human life is all about — a matter of opening oneself to God's grace and serving his will. So Christian and secularist collide, not on the periphery of their thinking, but at the center. It is misleading to picture the Christian and the secularist as walking hand in hand until certain out-of-the-way questions are raised, at which point they part company. On the contrary, they start from different premises because they hold different doctrines of man — of what constitutes his well-being and what effects his undoing.

You will meet secularists who will assume that you can agree with them about almost everything except two matters: Is there a God up there? and Is there life after death? Over the answers to these two questions we are expected to disagree with them. But this is assumed scarcely to matter, since for practical purposes the question whether there is life after death involves a future that is unknowable. And the dispute over what there is or is not up there plainly leaves us free to agree perfectly about what there is down here.

Many Christians have been infected by this kind of thinking. They are ready to accept that their faith affects their personal moral behavior, but for the life of the intellect, the thought-patterns that dominate attitudes in the multifarious business of work and play — this is something that they can share with secularists on equal terms. Theology, the science that ought to be giving a supernatural dimension to all our thinking, practical and theoretical, is assumed to be a matter of studying the nature of a God comfortably remote from most daily earthly affairs.

But in actual fact if you begin to read books of Christian theology — other than those produced by the trendy secularizers of our time — you soon find that before long you are involved in something with an immediate day-to-day bearing on what you think and say and do. Its effect is not to line you up with the secularist but to separate you from him. That is because, though "theology" technically means study of the nature of God, the nature of God, for the Christian, cannot be separated from the word of God and the works of God. And of course the word of God contains more about man than about God, more about human history than about events outside time. Even Milton's *Paradise Lost*, with its vast portrayals of heaven and hell, gives us a heaven and a hell where attention is focused upon this world and the life lived in it. Even the doctrine of the Trinity is in large part about God's relationship with men. God the Father is the creator of our world; God the Son is the redeemer of our world; God the Holy Spirit the comforter of our world. The doctrine of creation is about the making of our world; the doctrine of redemption about saving our world; the doctrine of the Holy Spirit about God's continuing activity in our world; the doctrine of grace about how we can function properly as human beings, as God's children. An awful lot of theology is about the kind of creatures we are and the kind of life we ought to live.

With this flood of distinctive supernaturally-orientated analysis of our human situation bearing down upon us as Christians, how can we possibly expect to jog on at the side of secularists in spheres like education as though we were together engaged on more or less the same task? We are not — except in the sense that we can formulate our common purpose in massively ambiguous sentences like: "We are concerned in education to nurture our pupils to fully human living" which blurs the fact that what being "fully human" amounts to is one thing to secularists and another thing to Christians. Nevertheless we get by in education by forever formulating statements about developing individuality and personality, potentiality and creativity, understanding and imagination — the Christian meaning one thing and the secularist meaning another so that common statements of purpose and policy are really trick sentences compounded by enormous puns. How could they be otherwise — when the human vocation, in Christian terms, is to be the child of God and an inheritor of the kingdom of heaven, while the human vocation in secular terms is to be the product of Nature and a bubbling fount of her unregenerate energies?

There is no escaping the fact that education is about being human and Christianity is about being human too, and any parallel definitions of what that means, as things now stand, would be stark mutual antitheses. In the eyes of modern educationists, we can scarcely fail to be human, for the nurtured seed that fructifies within us is willy-nilly our native endowment. The Christian view is that we have considerable difficulty in achieving the human status — the status of obedient divine affiliation. It is one of the freedoms of man that he can succeed in being human or fail to be so. This distinguishes him from lower animals. An animal can never betray its animality as we betray our humanity. G.K. Chesterton once observed that you might clap a fellow human being on the back if he was going to the dogs by drinking too much, and say, "Be a man!" but that there would be no point in urging a recalcitrant crocodile to be a crocodile.

For the Christian, life is a matter of salvation or damnation, and the truly human vocation is the former. For the Christian, life is a matter of living in a fallen world but a redeemed world, of inheriting a fallen nature but a divinely redeemed nature, of being thrust thus into cosmic conflict between the powers of evil and the powers of good. The contrast between Christian presuppositions and secularist ones could scarcely be greater. The Christian, by virtue of the revelation his Christian profession commits him to, sees all human life and human history held in the hands of God. That is what the Bible is all about. And this is the framework within which the Christian makes his estimate of all purpose and meaning down to the merest detail of act and thought. This life in nature of the senses and the brain is not the total sum of things. Overriding the vast machinery of historic and cosmic change stretches out the unchanging order of things supernatural where there is no need of sun and moon, for the glory of the Lord is all in all.

Whether the Christian reader nods in agreement or shakes his head because the rhetoric seems to outreach the simplicity of things, he will at least concede that here we touch a conceptual world into which the secularist never enters. For the secularist, this world of breathing and eating, calculating and measuring, getting and spending, flourishing and fading, aging and dying, is the total sum of things. For the secularist, talk of "purpose" or "meaning," "end" or "cause" relates to what has been done on this planet or what can be done on this planet (or the newly accessible ones) by the planet's own natural products, manipulating its resources with their five senses and their five wits within the straitjacketing dimension called "time." For the materialist there is nothing else. There is no other order of being than the visually and tangibly knowable. There is no extra-finite source from which a fingerweight of direction can be laid on the soul of man, a featherweight of influence on the affairs of man. Still less is there conceivably an order superior to time and place from which a supernatural incursion might be made by forces of good or evil, an order of being from which a divine entry might be made among the children of men.

Such is the measure of collision between Christian and secular thinking. I do not know what scale of measurement is used for gauging the force of impact when bodies collide, when bumper meets bumper on the highway, or I might utilize a graphic metaphor in trying to bring home the magnitude of the clash between the Christian mind and the secular mind. The clash is so violent that if we are not feeling bruised and battered when we reel back from our latest journey into "co-operation" with secularism over such areas of action as education, then we are probably losing sight of our Christian obligations. When Christian spokesman and secularist spokesman meet over fundamental human issues, there should be more than dented fenders and cracked windshield. For the meeting is between one who thinks that life is a matter of progress from vaccination to superannuation in a welfare society with wall-to-wall protection against discomfort and strain, and one who believes that we are pilgrims of eternity, molding souls on their way to everlasting life, and that our task is to bring fellow men and women into the company and keeping of the God who made them, visited them, and died for them. If the Christian view is as serious as that, it can never be peripheral to our lives; it must be central. There is nothing else that weighs by comparison with it.

"Why then," you might reasonably ask, "are you sitting in a comfortable room penning what you appear to regard as choice phrases on pieces of paper, if you feel like that? Ought you not to be knocking on doors and asking your fellow citizens if they are saved?" And if I reply, "I'm doing my best to enunciate the Christian message in such a way that it reaches the maximum number of fellow creatures," you might counter, "Ah, but you don't appear to have spent your life preaching the gospel. You chose to work in the field of education, which you seem to think pretty poorly of."

The objection is a serious one, but I maintain that there is an urgent need for Christians to work in secular fields of action. If all thinking Christians forsake all secular fields of action to turn full-time evangelist, the chasm between the Church and our secular civilization will become unbridgeable. Never was there greater need for Christian witness within our secular structures. In a talk on "Christianity and Literature"* C.S. Lewis said, "But the Christian knows from the outset that the salvation of a single soul is more important than the production and preservation of all the epics and tragedies in the world." That is a Christian truism perhaps. But it did not prevent Lewis from living the life of a literary man and teaching students all about those epics and tragedies. And indeed, doing so, he exerted an enormous influence on generations of students far wider than that of most pedagogues. And it is precisely by operating in fields of study like Literature or History or Physics that Christians can keep the Christian consciousness alive in these fields. Only the practice of Christian infiltration can whittle away the empire of secularism from within; this is the proper and effective response to that secularist infiltration which erodes morale within the Church.

It is interesting that in the same talk, quoted above, Lewis makes one point which illustrates very neatly and forcefully how the Christian will operate in a specialist field of study like that of English Literature to overturn secularist assumptions:

> What are the key-words of modern criticism? *Creative*, with its opposite *derivative; spontaneity*, with its opposite *convention; freedom*, contrasted with *rules*. Great authors are innovators, pioneers, explorers; bad authors bunch in schools and follow models. Or again great authors are always "breaking fetters" and "bursting bonds." They have personality, they "are themselves." I do not know whether we often think out the implication of such language into a consistent philosophy; but we have a general picture of bad work flowing from conformity and discipleship, and of good work bursting out from certain centres of explosive force—which we call men of genius.

Having thus defined the presuppositions embodied in current critical vocabulary, Lewis then goes on to show how New Testament thinking runs in the opposite direction. The highest good of crea-

---

* Published in *Rehabilitations*, 1939.

tures is to be creaturely—imitative. Originality belongs to God. The New Testament leaves no room for the current concept of "creativeness."

> Our whole destiny seems to lie in the opposite direction, in being as little as possible ourselves, in acquiring a fragrance that is not our own but borrowed, in becoming clean mirrors filled with the image of a face that is not ours.

"Clean mirrors filled with the image of a face that is not ours." The Christian mind is here operative in the world of culture and it produces an ideal of human quality contrary to ways of thinking still current in popular psychological theory.

Yet who can deny that, even more today than in Lewis's day, the vocabulary of educationists and psychologists, literary men and historians, presupposes precisely the anti-Christian ideal of human quality which Lewis here assaults. For it is not just the language of literary criticism that relies upon an ideal of human quality contrary to New Testament thinking. The very same ideal is implicit in the thinking that dominates our educational world. If one were to push further the kind of analysis of terminology Lewis enters upon in this paper, one would find a metaphorical system prevalent in the usage of current literature about artistic and educational activities that smashes the "clean mirror" to fragments. Artistic composition and educational development are alike often handled verbally in terms of an upsurge of animal instincts and the snapping of restraints upon restless inner urges—whether physical or emotional. (The metaphors implicitly link man with the animal world, evoking imagery of bestial desire let loose in primitive passion and self-assertion.) Or artistic composition and educational development are handled verbally in terms of involuntary growth like that in a garden: the seed, nurtured by environment, buds, sprouts and flowers into the full-grown glory of a masterpiece, the full-grown glory of human maturity. (The metaphors implicitly link man with the vegetable world, evoking imagery of plant life pushing upwards to the sun, impelled by virtue of its own innate expansiveness, and passively receptive to the refreshing environmental nutrition of rain and breeze.) Or artistic composition and educational development are handled verbally in terms of volcanic eruption. In the uneasy deeps of man's subconscious underworld, currents of emotion and traumatic association merge and coalesce into an uprush of streaming energy. (The metaphors implicitly link man with the mineral world, evoking imagery of volcanic action or of oil wells spurting out treasure from the earth's dark interior.)

This topic might merit further exploration were it not that the point at issue was fully developed in my book, *Repair the Ruins* (Reflections on Education from the Christian Point of View), published in 1950. Certainly we are now beset on all sides by psychological, educational, sociological, and historical—not to say popular scientific—commentary on the human scene that relies largely on metaphorical usage linking man inescapably and finally to the world of Nature, confining him within the deterministic system to which evolved animals, vegetables, and mineral deposits belong. We are losing that metaphorical vein (tapped by Lewis in the quoted sentences) which links man with the supernatural, which sees human vocation, not in terms of the animal, the vegetable, and the mineral, but in terms of "clean mirrors" that can be "filled with a face that is not ours."

The case is being made here that we Christians think and speak in an environment (a humanly contrived environment) in which the very phrases that spring most readily to our lips are soaked in metaphors which ground our thinking, openly or furtively, in naturalistic, deterministic, and mechanistic philosophies. Often when we think we are being most purely objective—most impartially "scientific" and factual—we are merely exchanging the metaphors that belong to an age-old view of the universe which allowed for the supernatural, for metaphors that belong to the philosophies of unregenerate secularism.

I made some analysis in my book, *The Faith and Modern Error*, of the way the terminology in which mental health and social well-being are described today bypasses any possible allowance for the supernatural criteria of divine vocation and eternal destiny. If we analyze the jargon utilized in current evaluation of personality and behavior, we shall find it grounded in naturalistic standards of earthly well-being that preclude any transcendent perspective.

An article appeared in the London *Times* not long ago by David

Martin, Professor of Sociology at the London School of Economics, a Christian who has not hesitated to bring the force of the Christian mind to bear upon current issues, notably perhaps in the controversy over linguistic up-dating of the liturgy. And though that indeed is the main issue in the particular article, a parenthetical observation sheds light on the wider question now before us. Lamenting recent desecration of rich liturgies and replacement by new designs reflecting "the thrust of organizational merger," Professor Martin sees the changes as "rooted in the fashions of the 1960s" and goes on:

> It is easy to recognize those *Bien pensant* misconceptions of self-hood and creativity which have damaged millions of young people, especially in America. The cult of spontaneity erases the frames and intimate spaces in which the self may grow. It disturbs the balance between subjective attention and the massive objectivity of the rite.

Now though Professor Martin's thoughts are primarily on the liturgical question, it is plain that he touches on a much wider issue in his assault upon the "cult of spontaneity." The "massive objectivity of the rite" is not the only massive objectivity disturbed by the dangerous subjectivity here under attack. The "frames and intimate spaces in which the self may grow" are being erased not only by ill-thought-out liturgical experiments but by ill-thought-out educational practices. For plainly the question of the proper balance between subjective attention and the once recognized "objectivities" of creed and rite, doctrine and word, priesthood and sacrament, is not in the last resort separable from the question of the proper balance between subjective attention and the "objectivities" of authority and form, duty and discipline, truth and wisdom, once recognized theoretically (if often questioned in practice) in the spheres of educational, political, and industrial life.

There will be more to be said about this matter when we turn to the defense of authority and the defense of reason, two massive objectivities currently under attack. The Church, like society at large, is under assault from forces that, by decomposing our objectivities and undermining our stabilities, are preparing the way for the triumph of evil. It is no accident that marriage, the family, the disciplined school, the ordered syllabus, the testing examination, are all under attack from within at the same time as creed and doctrine, tradition and wisdom, and all the objectivities that call out duty or deference, effort or discipline in social, political, and cultural spheres generally. The man who cannot see the Devil's fingers at work in the network of movements that would erode the standards and values of our Western civilization is stark blind. And the man who protests: "But so much of this is being done in the name of Christianity" should be told: "Exactly. That is how the Devil works. If you don't keep your wits about you—more than that, if you don't cling to the tried objectivities with all your might and main—in the end you don't know whether the great *Him* you serve and worship is God or the Devil himself." Try reading C.S. Lewis' *The Silver Chair* or *The Last Battle* in the light of this observation. Are not Lewis' Narnia stories a penetrating and prophetic commentary on where the trends of the 1960s were sure to lead? Who reigns? That is the question now. Whose voice is heard in the latest decision of synod, the latest theological best-seller? Is it really God's? Or has the ape dressed up the ass as the divine Lion?

Does all this sound hysterial? Consider how the vocabulary of delusive nihilism has crept from the secular into the Christian world—from lecture-room and platform to pulpit and parsonage, from secular press to religious press—when the very matter already touched on is at issue, the ideal of human quality. On all sides we hear echoes of the voguish pseudo-ethic which solemnly proclaims that a man must become a person (as though he were in danger of turning into a cabbage or a candlestick), that a man must learn to be himself (as though he lived under perpetual threat of being metamorphosed into his mother-in-law), that a man must seek and discover his identity (as though it were buried in the garden or hidden away in the attic), that a man must learn to accept himself for what he is, to find himself, to do his own thing, and so on. These clichés are here treated flippantly because, even on their own terms as secularist prescriptions and without reference to Christian judgments, they are totally evasive of real thought, utterly bereft of those "objectivities" in which standards and values, indeed even the concepts of good and evil, are grounded. They exemplify the linguistic and intellectual permissiveness which matches our current moral condition by obliteration of signpost and destination from the pilgrimage of life. They are indeed specimens of tautology, of verbal incest – the currency of non-thought in whose articulation terms and concepts feed upon each other in a closed circle.

But the Christian's objection to this new illiteracy touches deeper levels of revulsion than mere contempt for the morally moribund and intellectually inane. For in the Christian's eyes these clichés are the Devil's tags, the catch-phrases of hell. They virtually define damnation. For what is damnation except precisely the achievement of such selfhood as they recommend – the condemnation of a man to be exactly himself, nothing better than himself, a self untransfigured and untranscended for all eternity? What is damnation but that? The refusal to be born again. And what is the gospel call to live in Christ all about if there are no fallen selves to conquer, transcend, redeem – but just a lot of egos hanging about, waiting to be savored, explored, and revelled in exactly as they irremediably and irredeemably are? What of the call to put on the Lord Jesus Christ – to transform ourselves, as someone put it, into so many little Christs? That, one always understood, was the Christian's vocation.

The gist of this chapter is that the *differentiae* of Christianity, the characteristics of our faith which non-Christians do not share, are always the aspects of the faith which require emphatic recall. And at the present time the Christian doctrine of man, the Christian view of his nature, his vocation, and his destiny, is so alien to prevalent thinking in the spheres of public affairs and educational pursuits that it is the last thing Christians can afford to be forgetful of in their confrontation with others. Ours is no longer a world where the supernatural basis of things natural is generally allowed for. The fact comes forcefully home to us when we read the literature of the past. In the first Elizabethan age, writers catered naturally for a public with whom the supernatural perspective upon life could be taken for granted. Shakespeare wrote for a public in whose minds this life was framed within another, this temporal world within an everlasting one. Macbeth, contemplating murder, has to take "the life to come" into his calculations. Hamlet, pondering suicide, has to take "the undiscovered country after death" into the reckoning.

Shakespeare himself, bidding farewell to his human career as verbal enchanter through the mouth of Prospero, concedes that "my ending is despair/Unless I be relieved by prayer."

But if Shakespeare's day differed from our own in being an age in which the Christian interpretation of the human situation was more intellectually alive, it also differed from our own in being an age when the Christian social conscience was less alert and effective. For society made few provisions for the poor, the unemployed, the crippled, the lunatic, and the delinquent comparable to those our society makes today. If the Christian could hold to his creeds less tried by doubts and ridicule than we are, his social conscience ought surely to have been more continuously disturbed than ours are likely to be by the immediate spectacle of misery and suffering in the lanes and on the doorstep.

And therefore, in spite of the fact that the poor are always with us, one doubts whether, in the West at least, the social gospel, the clamor for redistribution of wealth and for more widespread human entry upon technology-based privilege and pleasure, is really the most urgent need of the day.

Nor indeed is this the time for us to line ourselves up with the secularists in prescribing for human well-being in the educational or cultural fields. For in these areas there is an implicit philosophy of subjectivity in the air which every healthy Christian instinct rejects. There is no value in subjectivity. The attempt to pretend that there is such value issues in absurdity, the kind of absurdity exemplified by a recent radio discussion I heard on an obviously worthless new play. "Does it say something?" "Oh yes, it says something." Period. Says what? It has become unfashionable to raise the question. Utterance has become valuable in itself whether what is uttered is rationally worth hearing or not, indeed whether what is uttered is rationally intelligible or not. Oh yes, the writer says something. So what? Hitler said something—a good deal too much, one might argue. But considerations of meaning and value which would differentiate what Hitler said from what Einstein said are no longer applicable in the world of media subculture. "Here is a play that makes a statement, a very important statement." Period. You would be made to appear an old fuddy-duddy if you asked, "What kind of statement? True or false? Perceptive or obtuse? Wise or foolish?"

We shall turn later in this book to a fuller consideration of this new irrationality which is blinding a whole generation to the nature of things—the issue is precisely the *nature* of things, the ground base of fact and objectivity, of quality and reason, of relationship and connection, of grade and scale, inherent in God's created world for the discerning human mind that has operated to raise us from the jungle to the city. If our cities are now returning to the jungle it is because the new irrationality directs, not the "minds," but the wills of a growing tribe of young people deprived of the freedom which consists in being brought up in a world with signposts. Without signposts there is no freedom. Given the signposts, you can make your choice; you can go either toward London or toward Edinburgh, either toward New York or toward Los Angeles; you can go South or North, East or West; and you can go either toward Vanity Fair or toward the Delectable Mountains. Without signposts there is only the compulsion of untutored whim, and compulsion is slavery.

The new slavery into which Western man is being dragged by the influence of media, education, and the "intellectual" barbarians who mold public thinking is a slavery based on the biggest contrick since Satan presented an apple to Eve. And the issues at stake are almost as momentous.

3

Where do we stand against the denigration of authority?

WE HEAR ON all sides that the modern crisis is a crisis of authority. This is notably true of the crises within the Christian Church and within the world of education. The potential convert to Christianity is invited to accept as valid a traditional interpretation of life's purpose which is rooted in God's revelation of himself to man in the figure of Christ. The validity of this interpretation is guaranteed by the Christian reading of the past, in which the hand and the person of God are seen historically at work, by the Christian reading of the nature of reality and of the human situation as explored by the faculty of reason, and by the Christian reading of personal testimonies from men and women living in the faith. This threefold guarantee of Christian orthodoxy by history, reason, and experience has been fully articulated by specialist scholars in various fields of historical, philosophical, and theological study. It would be pretentious to try to take a brief trip into any of these fields on a cheap half-day excursion, but it would be evasive to pretend that the problem of authority is not a taxing one.

Here we must make clear that the central problem of authority is not a question about who lays down external rules and exercises control; it is a question of asserting standards and attesting purposes. The question, Who leads the expedition? is secondary to the question, Are there any maps or compasses? What about the erection and labelling of those signposts on which civilization and personal progress depend? This is the problem of authority — the authority of orthodoxy. Are we going to label the signposts with the names of towns which long experience and the testimony of maps suggest would be the right ones? Or is this attitude too traditionalist and conformist, too paternalistic and authoritarian? Might it not be better to leave the signposts blank and allow the travellers the excitement of discovering for themselves what lies ahead? Surely we do not want a generation brought up with closed minds — accepting without question what the signposts tell them? Much better the open-ended attitude which leaves the signposts blank. Enough of the glib authoritarianism that declares such and such a road to be the route to London; after all, I may want to turn off at Grantham, so for me it will be the road to Melton Mowbray. There are no easy answers to the question, Where does this road lead?

The kind of nonsense exemplified above has not yet been applied to the signposts on our roads — only to our moral, intellectual, and cultural signposts. We shall probably not allow the anarchy about signposting and direction to spread to our road system because commercial interests would be affected and money would be lost; whereas the obliteration of moral, cultural, and spiritual signposts does damage only to minds and souls. The standard of living remains unimpaired.

There is a stage of educational development at which perhaps Ian Fleming seems more entertaining than Shakespeare and Sullivan more tunefully attractive than Bach. The young pupil grows to maturity of taste in so far as he distrusts his own first-hand judgments in these matters (which would prefer Fleming to Shakespeare and Sullivan to Bach) and gives the benefit of the doubt to the traditional literary or musical orthodoxy, patiently — perhaps in some respects arduously — training his understanding to the point at which he too not only accepts *on authority* that Shakespeare and Bach are worthy of the maximum attention and veneration in their respective fields, but can also personally testify to the validity of the orthodox evaluation. Education is rooted in deference to authority.

A distinguished statesman has recently observed, with apparent approval, that the age of "deference" has gone. If it has, then civilization is doomed. One can go further. If deference has gone, then civilization has already disappeared. For "deference" before the authority of the orthodoxies which teach us how to use our mother tongue, in what order to employ the symbols, 1, 2, 3, and 4, which berries you can eat and which you had better leave alone, and on which side of the road you should drive your car — such deference alone guarantees the continuance of civilization and of life itself.

Some readers may object that the words "authority" and "deference" are here being used in a way very different from the usage of the disparagers of the concepts. But one of the key ways in which the minds of our people are being corrupted and their values destroyed is precisely by the technique of repeatedly emphasizing only the pejorative connotations of certain terms until the public, forgetting the ameliorative connotations, writes off concepts as invalid just because certain select connotations appropriate to the concepts have been discredited. If we use "deference" only to mean "obsequiousness," or something of the kind, then we can easily persuade people that they would be better off without it. But if we want to flatter ourselves that we have got rid of obsequiousness (and anyone who has seen media-interviewers cringing before film directors or fashion designers would dispute the claim) why seize the opportunity to denigrate "deference," a vastly different thing? Civilization depends on the fact that the ignorant pupil must defer to his instructor in the classroom, the motorist must defer to the policeman, the writer must defer to the dictionary on his shelf. All these — instructor, policeman, and dictionary — are in their various spheres "authorities" to whom or which fit "deference" is due. A substantial book could be written about the assault upon vocabulary by which the current disintegration of civilization is engineered. Pejorative connotations are attributed exclusively to words which in fact can accommodate quite other connotations ("defer," "authority," "discrimination," "traditional," and "dogmatic" are cases in point) and people's minds are bereft of concepts and terms essential to the health of our culture.

Let us consider a few sentences from a sermon preached in the early 1960s by a distinguished churchman at a time when the challenge to Christian authority was perhaps at its strongest:

> This is a day of uncertainty. In some quarters it is more fashionable to air doubts than to declare convictions. This does not help those who are floundering. No easy authoritarianism, however, will do. To say "The Bible says," or "The Church says," is of no avail. On the other hand, a personal faith, thought out, worked out, and prayed out, carries an authority of its own.

This passage is selected, not because it unambiguously merits criticism, but because it neatly puts on display the terms we need to consider. They are here operative in a characteristically fashionable mode. If we probe the speaker's usage, we shall first note that he uses the terms "authoritarianism" when he wants to convey the idea of authoritativeness as a bad or unacceptable thing, and "authority" when he wants to convey the idea of authoritativeness as a good thing. One can have no quarrel with this practice; it is useful and appropriate. But surely one must be perturbed to see "authoritarianism" (as a bad thing) associated with the teaching of the Bible or the Church, and "authority" (as a good thing) associated with the evidence of personal testimony. This distribution of terms is tendentious, arbitrary, and, in the last analysis, prejudicial to rational judgment.

The thesis of this chapter would turn the tables on the above usage. Authority is the only thing that can save us from authoritarianism; and with this point our preacher would concur. But, in our view, *authority* attaches essentially to the impersonal, to the collective tradition, while *authoritarianism* attaches essentially to the personal individual will. If a man says to me, "You can't park your car there. The law forbids it. It's a no-parking zone," I would not accuse him of authoritarianism but of a proper deference to authority. But if he says, "You can't park your car there because I won't permit it," then the case is altered. He is being what I call "authoritarian." One is prepared to listen with due respect to the man who says, "The law lays down..." One is not prepared to listen with comparable respect to the man who says, "I'm telling you...." Authority saves us from authoritarianism. The public mind in our generation has been confused and misled precisely by concealment of the fact that in religion, in education, in the life of society generally, it is authority that saves us from authoritarianism. It is respect for the central orthodoxies of law, culture, and religion that alone preserves us from a multiplicity of intolerable petty authoritarianisms exercised by those who have the loudest voices, the strongest arms, or the most assertive egos.

Thus, to say "The Bible says" or "The Church teaches" is of compelling weight for the very reason that the speaker is *not* being authoritarian. He is not even saying that he, as an individual, necessarily fully understands, fully agrees. He is presenting the truly authoritative voice of the Scriptures as heeded and reverenced by intelligent Christians for two thousand years, or of the Church as summing up in its teaching the collective wisdom of learned and simple men alike over the same period. There is a lot to be said for the man who withdraws his personal authority from his utterance—or at least submerges it; the man whose words and actions together say (implicitly, of course) "Don't pay any great attention to *my* opinions. They are neither here nor there. I expect that, like others, I get plenty of things wrong anyway. But the Bible says this, or the Church says that; and in so far as I've found the way of peace or of fruitful action it has been in deference to this body of teaching. There it is. Let it speak for itself. Look at it for yourself. It has done a lot for me."

This attitude represents the dead antithesis of authoritarianism precisely because it gives the full weight of value and significance to the teaching of the Bible or of the Church. The speaker refuses to pose as a testifier—except to the objective thing outside himself. He insists on assuming the role of fellow-seeker, listening at your side (not *telling* you) to the voice of collective tradition. He grants that tradition its authority, and is thereby enabled to step personally into the background, to direct eyes and attention to something other and far greater than himself.

Now I do not wish to imply for a moment that the preacher whose words I quoted meant to recommend attitudes utterly inconsistent with the attitude I am recommending. My point is that his words might well lend color to the kind of subjectivism and personalism from which our age suffers. His paragraph was cited primarily because it allowed convenient investigation of certain words in action, and such analysis leaves one wishing that he had taken care to check (rather than to be in danger of encouraging) current drifts in linguistic usage that tend to disparage authority.

Authoritarianism essentially consists in advertising the self as authority or as a unit in a fabric of authority with overbearing weight. In so far as collective traditions are given authoritative priority, the self can be withdrawn. Thus in religion, as in law and as in education, the formal authority (perhaps institutionalized) of the continuing central tradition is alone what preserves us from thousands of petty individual authoritarianisms. And those in the religious field, as in education, who would try to lead others to assume automatic priority of individual assertion over the continuing tradition are not helping the cause of religion or of culture generally. They may speak in the name of "sincerity," of "vitality," of "freshness," of "newness," of "creativity" — and conversely try to discredit notions of formal authority by the use of pejorative adjectives. It is important to bring sharp discernment to bear upon such utterances, discernment that can penetrate beneath the emotive slants and detect the dangerous recommendation of opinionated individualism over against collective wisdom. Special watchfulness is required in this respect to match a special danger; for any day one may hear statements which discredit the authority of Bible or Church from people whose degree of understanding would scarcely justify them in questioning the credentials of a hack journalist.

One must not fail to observe, however, that orthodoxy, just as much as heresy, can be defended by an individual authoritarianism that makes one sick. If any attitude is authoritarian, it is *ipso facto* not truly authoritative. The genuinely authoritative is that which relies upon authority, and not upon authoritarianism. "I have grave doubts about the Virgin Birth," as a pulpit statement, smacks of authoritarianism, since it invites the natural and proper response, "And who are you to have doubts about it anyway?" Likewise, "I can assure you that the Virgin Birth is a fact," as a pulpit statement, is another instance of authoritarianism if the "I" is asserted as a decisive element in the sentence, giving it force and establishing its credentials. Who am *I* to know or not to know? I can only repeat the assertions of others in this matter. But the statement, "The Bible teaches us — or the Church teaches us — that our Lord was born of the Virgin Mary" is not only authoritative, it is unquestionably true, utterly irrefutable. That *is* what the Bible and the Church teach. Even unbelievers would not deny it. And considering the respect in which the teaching of Bible and Church have been held for hundreds of years, and the millions of people of highest intelligence, knowledge and understanding who have given this teaching the status of maximum authoritativeness, it is surely untimely to urge now — as our quoted preacher does — that to say "The Bible says" or "The Church says" is of little avail. If indeed this were true, we should want to know what *is* of avail. We must be wary indeed of any encouragement of the notion that more reliable than Bible or Church is the voice of any individual hot-gospeller who chooses to stand on a soap box and proclaim, "Look at me, the living advertisement of the truth!"

This is not to say that the preacher we quoted intended anything so absurd as this. We are not trying to associate him by innuendo with any such view. We are saying that a given situation demands of the Church an appropriate counterbalancing emphasis, and that the given situation at the present time requires from the Church the discrediting of the subjective in favor of the objectively authoritative. In religion, as in education, it is an urgent matter that all we who teach should recapture the attitude, "Let us look at this thing together, you and I." Then "this thing," whatever it is, should be allowed to speak. That is the sound approach whether "this thing" is a play of Shakespeare's or a law of physics or the doctrine of the Incarnation. In any such sphere the perpetual intrusion of the interfering "I" (*I* think this; *I* think that; *I* feel this; *I* feel that; *I* like this; *I* don't like that) is a nuisance and, more often than not, an impediment to the spread of understanding and appreciation. Elucidation of the objective, rather than the endless airing of ill-considered superficial judgments tossed between numbers of people all more or less equally unequipped to judge, is the need of the hour, the way back to cultural health—indeed the way back to mental health. For people are crying out for the nourishment of it. (As anyone who has taught in higher education during the last twenty years is aware, people may not know in advance what it is that they are crying out for; but once the real food is provided, they are eager to admit how famished they have been.)

We argue that you do not teach the Resurrection on the strength of your own authority any more than you teach the Second Law of Thermodynamics on the strength of your own authority. Such doctrines are matters which you present to your audience or your pupils on the basis of an authority so massive that you yourself, *qua* preacher or teacher, are microscopically insignificant to the extent that an attempt to give yourself a weighty place in the validating of the doctrine would be laughably absurd. It would also of course be breathtakingly presumptuous. You present these doctrines as having behind them the community of believers (the Church) and the community of science respectively. You present them as doctrines, therefore, which you, as a disciple, in either the community of believers or the community of science, stand before with bowed head, calling other disciples to stand before them likewise at your side. You stand, not claiming to know all, but attesting the proven reliability of the doctrines in terms of brains and lives much superior to your own. Where you feel yourself wishing to say, "I disagree," you restrain yourself, because of the weight of authority against you. You are more inclined to say, "This part I cannot understand fully yet" or "I've not yet been able to see how this fits in with the rest" than to say, "Of course this bit is nonsense." In short you give orthodoxy the benefit of the doubt. It is obvious that the attempt to turn everyone into an opinionated know-all in the field of Christian theology or in any other field is a move towards anarchy.

In reply to this case it will be argued, no doubt, that it represents an oversimplification because we no longer have a central orthodoxy in Christian theology but rather a variety of rival views. This possible reply needs to be analyzed, for it is widely used for the purpose of discrediting orthodoxy.

It must be accepted that we cannot use any statistical device for determining what Christians essentially believe. Christianity, like most things in this error-ridden world, is more generally misunderstood than understood. This situation obtains in other areas of culture. The fact that fewer people in the world enjoy and understand the music of Bach than fail to do so does not prevent musical "orthodoxy" from making the highest claims for his genius and from giving him the fullest attention in the musical encyclopedias, textbooks, and courses of musical study. Orthodoxy is not necessarily numerically preponderant. Indeed, as Kierkegaard says, "The crowd is untruth." If the situation in the sphere of Christian teaching were as chaotic as many people would have us believe, then the compilation of (authoritative) encyclopedias of the Christian Faith, covering central doctrines and practices, would be impossible. But in fact such encyclopedias exist, offering clear definitions and no less clear demarcations distinguishing what is central and orthodox from what has been taught by deviants.

The Christian Church is perhaps the one body in the world which can claim an unchallengeable orthodoxy for the very reason that, by definition, by virtue of its own essential character, it is a body that bestrides the centuries and, as such, does not require any calculation of what Christians alive on this planet at this particular moment happen to think before declaring its orthodoxies. They have been proclaimed in Scripture and Creed. If "Christians" today happened to disagree with some of those propositions or tenets, that would not mean that Christianity would have to be defined differently; it would mean that those supposed "Christians" would have to be reminded that they are not Christians after all. It is too late to change Christianity. You cannot now fabricate a theory, a belief, as being Christian if it goes against the professed beliefs of the Christians of the last two thousand years, whether they are known teachers like St. Paul or St. Augustine or St. Thomas Aquinas, or unknown men and women who simply said their prayers and their creed and died in their faith. You cannot exclude your ancestors in the faith from the full understanding of what the faith really is. If anyone knew, St. Paul knew and St. Augustine knew and St. Thomas knew.

One can go further. An attempt to *change* Christian belief can spring only from an anti-Christian impulse, for it represents an attempt to betray a great body of men and women who have lived and died for the very thing you would tamper with. Indeed it may be said, in these times of troubled understandings and corrupted judgments, that nothing differentiates the genuine Christian from the would-be eroder of the faith more surely than the Christian's mental involvement with a body of believers on two sides of the grave.

A distinguished statesman was asked by a journalist what made him a Christian. He replied that the death of his mother had been crucial in convincing him of the life hereafter. He could not believe her extinguished. When C.S. Lewis wrote about his response to the news of Charles Williams' death, he said, "When the idea of death and the idea of Williams met in my mind, it was the idea of death that was changed." Awareness of the living dead goes deep in the Christian consciousness. What is the doctrine of the Resurrection all about if not that death is swallowed up? And if we seriously believe that death is swallowed up, we shall reckon with our continuing kinship with our fellows beyond the grave. For Christians there is no such thing as shaking off the past (the communal past; repenting of the individual past is a different matter). In another context C.S. Lewis wrote: "Humanity does not pass through phases as a train passes through stations: being alive, it has the privilege of always moving yet never leaving anything behind. Whatever we have been, in some sort we are still." The Church has always recognized the involvement of our forbears in acts of worship. Therefore with angels and archangels and with all the company of heaven, we laud and magnify thy glorious name. That is characteristic of how a historic liturgy speaks. One is tempted to take up a familiar current cliché. "That is what Christianity is all about." One has heard it used of ministering to the poor and needy, of spreading neighborliness and good fellowship, of answering the needs of the Third World. Indeed, the sentence can be validly—if not exclusively or comprehensively—used in these contexts. These are some of the things that Christianity is all about. But it is also—and perhaps overridingly—about the fact that the past is not dead, that our deceased friends and relations are not extinguished, that our ancestors in the faith live still.

This fact lends a peculiar weight and force in Christendom to tradition. "Tradition" is another much misused word, often applied glibly to the persistence of certain rather unnecessary habits and ceremonies left over from days when things were done differently. "Tradition" is a much bigger word than pejorative journalistic use of the term allows for. For instance, our arithmetical system of calculating is a tradition. We are being traditionalists whenever we use this numerical scale handed down from the past. The language we speak is a tradition; the meanings it conveys are traditional. These also are things that have been handed down to us—with all the built-in concepts of value and quality that mean so much to us. So we are being traditionalists whenever we speak. You cannot say, "This is good" or "That is bad" without committing yourself to acceptance of an ancient tradition. If a man wants to break with tradition in this respect he will find it difficult. Suppose he makes the effort and says, "When I say a thing is *good*, I don't mean that it ought to be approved of; I mean that the less we have of it, the better," he might think he was being pretty radical here. But in fact it is a poor attempt because, except for the word *good*, he has used every word in the sentence in the traditional manner. He has relied wholly upon the machinery of tradition in trying to break away from tradition. And indeed every anti-traditionalist movement that ever took off in human history was something wholly dependent upon the acceptance of tradition for making its points at the supposed expense of tradition.

One might argue that life is too short to indulge much anti-traditionalism. Languages and systems of meaning; numbers and systems of calculation—these traditional things are not made in a day. (And, incidentally, they are not the invention of barbaric half-wits by whom the world in ancient days is sometimes assumed to have been inhabited.) Tradition is threaded through our daily lives and thoughts from moment to moment, and it is not peculiar to Christians to be attached to it.

Yet Christianity gives a special salt to our in-built dependence upon tradition by its insistence that past individuals live still in their own right as well as in the generally accepted continuity of their thoughts and ways with ours. G.K. Chesterton once neatly summed up what this means. "Tradition may be defined as an extension of the franchise. Tradition means giving votes to that most obscure of all classes, our ancestors." Variation in degree of personal sensitivity to this extension of franchise accounts for the deep feeling which is stirred by current controversy over such matters as reforming liturgies, remodelling ethics, ordaining women, and so on. The Christian with a highly developed sense of his membership in a community that bestrides the centuries will kick against arguments that are based only on what Christians alive today happen to think, for such arguments disenfranchise their ancestors. And such Christians may think it unwise for innovators to argue for change on the basis of democratic ascendency. If you accept the "one man, one vote" principle for the Christian Church, the pollsters will have to do most of their opinion sampling in heaven; though there might be a few "don't knows" to check up on in less comfortable eternal regions. It is important for the great enthusiasts for democratic Christian procedures to bear this in mind. If you extend the franchise fully, as Chesterton would recommend, you can never put the traditionalists in a minority. They have a built-in majority from the past.

Surely we all have our favorite saints, heroes, and teachers of the past. Is it unreasonable to pause before making changes which cut us off from them and set the Church on a course which their thinking would seem to disallow? It is natural for the tradition-soaked Christian to pause when he reads some glib argument taking for granted the latest move in so-called "liberalization" and to ask, What would George Herbert or Lancelot Andrewes, John Wesley or Doctor Johnson say to that? If we hope to be with them in heaven, we must perhaps expect to be questioned by them and asked to account for what we did with what they bequeathed us. The prospect of being cross-questioned is perhaps enough to arouse apprehension even in formidable protagonists of change. As an Englishman, I have sometimes wondered who will volunteer in heaven to explain to Dr. Johnson the case for ordaining women; but then I have been assured by a woman that the very question arises from too masculine an angle, and that the feminine concept of heaven precludes the necessity of having to converse with Dr. Johnson.

To be serious again, there is no intention here to suggest that tradition is always infallible. It is not. But it is both uncivilized and unChristian to brush tradition roughly aside in heady accommodation to the spirit of the age. "Liberal" reformers need to recognize the deep-rooted character of our kinship with fellow-members of the Church now departed from this life. When we think of the caliber of their thought and witness, we are surely, if we are humble, compelled to give them as ready a hearing as tonight's voice on the telly or today's columnist in the newspaper.

The word "humble" is used here because Christian humility certainly demands a conscious deference before the collective wisdom of those forefathers from whom we have inherited the faith — with all its treasures of literature, scholarship, art, architecture, liturgy, rite, and institutional articulation. It is especially important to stress this because an emotive assault upon defenders of credal orthodoxy is often made nowadays that tries to associate their stand with pride and their opponents' lack of commitment with humility. A topsy-turvy argument has been propounded that defenders of traditional orthodoxy have the insufferable conceit to pretend to *know*, while liberals (and agnostics too for that matter) assume the humbler pose of seekers after truth who are not yet ready to claim the miraculous "certainties" that orthodoxy upholds.

The question at issue may be framed thus: Given the limitations of human understanding, is not agnosticism more humble than belief, and liberal questioning more humble than credal affirmation? The question arises from the plain fact that the finite cannot comprehend the infinite. Man's brain is such that it cannot adequately contain the idea of God. It is always grasping at the idea and failing to embrace it. It has to be content with images which fade before they are fully formed, with notions which evaporate before they are clearly conceptualized. In the effort to think of God, man's very apparatus of conceptualization is always straining and then breaking down. Faced with this difficulty, modern man is tempted to reach the conclusion that a permanent state of agnosticism is the correct posture for unpresuming mortals. Worse still, modern man is tempted to decry as presumptuous all past attempts by the Church to give clarity of outline to the image of God, to trace a definable divine personality in the acts by which he is alleged to have made himself known and available.

The view that the human mind cannot fully contain the idea of God is indisputable. But to turn this fact into an excuse for continuous agnosticism or that permanent tentative half-belief which passes itself off as liberal open-mindedness is neither logically sound nor morally wholesome. It is not difficult to argue that the degree of presumption inherent in questioning two thousand years of tradition is greater than that inherent in upholding it. I have already had something to say on this point in my *Defence of Dogmatism*, but there is still more to be said, and the issue is such a live one today in some circles that one need not apologize for returning to the theme and extending the previous case.

The objection against confident belief, full-blooded credal affirmation, which we are here concerned with is based on a confusion between genuine humility and bogus humility. There is no cause to analyze the character of genuine humility. There would be no quarrel on that score. But there are two distinct devices by which presumption can masquerade as humility, and both are brought unconsciously into play when men claim that agnosticism or tentative belief are humbler postures than firm orthodox commitment.

Let us look at these two devices, representing two faces on the coin of human self-deception. The first may be summed up by the sentence: An apparently modest disclaimer may reveal pretensions of unsuspected magnitude. To illustrate what this means in practice, let us imagine that a young man is learning to play the piano. After a year or two the teacher realizes that his pupil's musical ability is mediocre, his aural and neural gifts negligible, and his powers of application slight. Yet he encourages the pupil, noting that he is making some progress in the direction of being a humdrum accompanist for hymns in Sunday School. One day the young man says, with all the overtones appropriate to becoming modesty, "Of course it's going to be some time before *I* am in a position to play piano concertos with an orchestra. I'm not nearly ready yet." The pupil apparently thinks he is being unassuming. The teacher is astounded at the enormity of the self-conceit. "Not nearly ready yet!" That "yet" provides the most ironic touch of all.

Perhaps this example will help to reinforce the insistence of the orthodox believer that the man who witholds intellectual commitment on the grounds that we don't know enough about God "yet" is, by his very disclaimer, voicing secret pretensions of astonishing presumption. We don't know enough about God *yet*? Are our supposedly "humble" agnostics and liberals really serious in the use of that word *yet*? For the presupposition, if we take them seriously, is that the time will come when finite creatures *will* know enough on earth about their divine Creator to pronounce on his status, character, and deserts with well-corroborated confidence.

We said that there were two faces to the coin of human presumption in relation to this issue, and that is one of them. The other face can be discerned only after some effort of penetration. It must be granted that all admissions of personal limitedness which are genuine and do not cover enormous pretensions with a veil of disclaiming are appropriate in the response of the creature to the Creator. Recognition of the incapacity of the human mind to contain the idea of God is a healthy mark of self-knowledge, provided that it does not carry the implication that the human mind is only "as yet," in the twentieth century, inadequate to what is being asked of it *now*. For recognition of the incapacity of the human mind to contain the idea of God is *in itself* one thing, whereas the same recognition made the basis for suspension of action is another and very different thing. We have not manufactured our own brains; they were given to us. A recognition of their limitations, made the basis for limitation of human commitment, becomes virtually a *complaint* against their limitations and the Person who imposed them. In other words, the Creator-God gave us our brains, and if we say that they are not capable of *adequately* (given the finite scheme) doing now what God is asking of them, we are not humbly confessing our limitations but grandly telling God that he has not done his job properly. It must be granted that this distinction is a fine one; but then many crucial distinctions in the moral sphere are fine ones.

Let us look again at our analogy of the pianist. Let us suppose this time that our young student is an altogether different person in character and gifts. He makes prodigious progress, turns himself into a virtuoso, and is acclaimed throughout the world. A distinguished composer writes a new concerto specially for him. It is thoroughly rehearsed for weeks, but then on the eve of the first performance the pianist suddenly says to the composer, "No, I can't go forward with this." "But it is going splendidly," the composer protests. "You play it brilliantly. Surely you have not lost faith in me and my work." "It is not that," says the pianist. "Indeed the trouble is the exact opposite. I have the maximum respect for you and your work. I recognize the grandeur of this new conception. It is possibly the finest concerto ever written. You have gone deeper than any previous composer into the unfolding of whatever it is that lies at the heart of musical utterance. The conception outreaches any possible practical realization. It is too profound to be realized in execution. No strings are stringy enough, no brass brassy enough, no piano percussive enough to body your magnificent conception in sound. I would not insult you by trying. I revere too deeply the mysteries you have plumbed in this masterpiece. Goodnight."

Is this humility, this complaint that the instruments are inadequate to do justice to what is being asked of them, that the equipment at the performers' disposal is deficient in relation to the magnificent project in which they are asked to play their part?

If there is a God calling us, we cannot turn back on him with the reply that he has not given us a reliable enough machinery of recognition for us to be able to hear and identify his voice *just yet*. If there is a God demanding something of us, we cannot suspend action on the excuse that he has not yet given us a sure enough equipment of reception and understanding for us to be able to respond satisfactorily. If we do so respond, it is a response not of humility but presumption. Such conceit, such inertia, such negativity are open options for man in time. But belief and commitment represent a very different response which is at the same time more rational, more reverent, more humble, and more creaturely.

It is because an attack upon authority and tradition is so difficult to mount in rational terms that recourse is so often had by liberals and radicals to techniques of emotive smear such as the device just analyzed of falsely connecting the proclamation of credal truths with human self-conceit. The difficulty of attacking authority and tradition is the difficulty inherent in assaulting what is in effect the source and basis of your own weaponry of assault – the language you use and the rational equipment you employ. These are yours by virtue of the civilized human inheritance handed on to you from the past. And because the assault upon valid authority and tradition in principle must always, by virtue of this universal rational dependence upon them, be in danger of self-contradiction and therefore of nullity, all attempts to weaken the foundation of Christian orthodoxy tend to have recourse to denigration in lieu of substantial argument. If you cannot prove that deference to authoritative tradition is irrational, you can imply that it is conceited, unadventurous and cowardly, or complacent and smug, or narrow-minded and uncharitable.

It is a pity that theological controversy has to concern itself not just with countering rational argument but also—and today especially so—with answering innuendo, denigration, and abuse.

The most disreputable device of controversy is what is called the *argumentum ad hominem*, which is simply the switch from reasoning to personal abuse. Representations of quarrels in plays and novels tend to exploit this human weakness, sometimes for tragic, often for comic, effect. Husband and wife start by disagreeing about whether Johnny is old enough to be allowed to go alone to a football match. "But he's fourteen," says father. "Why at that age I was allowed to go where I pleased provided that I was back by nine o'clock." "Yes," the mother replies. "And look what kind of thing you got up to as a result." "Well, who are you to talk?" Before long the contestants are raking over each other's pasts and the question whether Johnny should be allowed to go to the match has been lost sight of.

It can make amusing entertainment on the stage or over the air, and at this level the recourse to personal abuse, the *argumentum ad hominem*, is easily recognized. So far as rational argument is concerned, it is a red herring; it solves no dispute; it forwards no case; it is a cheap and nasty way of venting one's anger at being opposed and not getting one's own way. But the very same device can be used at a sophisticated level and pass itself off as scholarship. And the world of theological controversy has had its atmosphere fouled during the past decade by recourse to this device. Instead of arguments being conducted to establish that such-and-such a view was false or logically untenable, we have been increasingly treated to statements and insinuations declaring the attachment to certain orthodox views as rooted in "unadventurousness," "cowardly resistance to change," "fear of the new," "love of security" and other psychological conditions that appear to merit contempt.

Now there are some parts of the world where holding Christian views at all may require courage as opposed to cowardice. But the notion that holding radical as opposed to traditional Christian views in modern Western society calls for courage as opposed to cowardice, adventurousness as opposed to love of security, and so on, is laughable. And it is evident testimony to the weakness of the liberals' case that they have to forsake rational argument and fall back repeatedly on emotive smears which, if they are examined, are self-evidently ridiculous.

But the device, however patently absurd, is used, and used sometimes with such superficial appearance of rational plausibility that its mechanisms need to be brought into the light of day. For. devious as the technique is, it has lately begun to assume an appearance of respectability. Thus a writer who disagrees with someone else's thesis will avoid tackling it honestly and openly, point by point, and say instead: "Now this thesis is very odd indeed, and we must examine carefully the psychological basis of opinions so extraordinary, to see if analysis can shed light on what it is that leads people to adopt views of this kind."

Now what has happened during the course of this sentence is that the writer has prepared the ground for a full-scale *argumentum ad hominem*, a wholesale recourse to personal abuse. "Let us examine the psychological basis that makes you hold such extraordinary views," is only another way of saying, "*You* are the one who needs to be examined, not your views!" In short, it is the academic's version of "You bloody fool!"

It is important that the glib ease of translating "You are a fool" into an apparently sober argument by recourse to the questionable jargon of psychology should be publicly exposed. A recent article in a London newspaper gave an account of a new book which is described as a thorough study of the conservative evangelical movement, its leaders, and its literature. In the book, the author accuses the movement "of exclusiveness, shallowness, rigidity and dishonesty." Now there is no intention here to pass comprehensive judgment upon an unread book, but only to pinpoint a method of argument increasingly used to discredit opponents. The newspaper article describes the author's case thus: He "regards the attraction of the fundamentalist-conservative evangelical position as being of psychological rather than religious origin (*sic*), the same mechanism that makes other allegedly sectarian groups a haven for those who need to feel different from and better than, the average person." At this level, if the article is fair to the author, we have reached the rock bottom of personal abuse masquerading as argument. For the "argument" may be justly paraphrased thus: "You evangelicals hold the beliefs you do because your vanity needs the boost of a false feeling of superiority to your fellows."

It is surely unwise to operate on this level of religious controversy. The *argumentum ad hominem* tends to propagate its kind parthenogenetically; it invites a come-back on its own terms. One is tempted to apply the device to the writer who has himself employed it, to make a psychological analysis of his peculiar need to make psychological analyses of people he happens to disagree with, and to examine carefully the psychological motivation for discrediting those who hold faith with infectious conviction. It is better to avoid these temptations, to look at the matter more objectively, and to ask, not, "What is it in the author's mentality that engenders this emotive antagoinsm?" but, "What is it in the conservative evangelical case that provokes this emotive opposition?"

We have already answered this question. If you take your stand on authority—the authority of traditional orthodoxy, the authority of the Scriptures, the authority of the Church—you make rational counterattack difficult in that all rationality and all utterance derive their validity from the authority of tradition. Rational response being difficult, controversialists are tempted to bring into play the machinery of irrational response—in this case the technique of denigration masquerading as psychological analysis.

It is interesting that the feverish passion for discrediting authority (which has invaded the Christian from the secular world) should now be producing good out of evil, by drawing together parties that have previously been at loggerheads. In England, a most notable instance of this is the way the liberal assault upon authority has drawn together those "Evangelical" and "Catholic" elements in the Church of England who have in the past confronted one another with attachment to the rival authorities of Bible and Church. In the assailants of all authority they have found a common foe and realized, with a jolt, that their allegiance to the "massive objectivities" of Bible and Church give them deep mutual understanding in the face of attack from subjectivists and relativists whose only authority resides in themselves.

I have just read some words publicly addressed by an Evangelical to an Anglo-Catholic. "Like you, we don't make it up as we go along." That puts in a nutshell the difference between those who accept authority and those whose course of thought is a continuing rebellion against it. When some aberrant theologians recently published a book attempting to revive the old Psilanthropic and Socinian heresies that deny Christ's divinity, it was the Evangelical Council that urged the authors of the book to resign their Anglican orders on the grounds that an ordained churchman had responsibility to teach the Church's doctrine. In receiving holy orders, the men in question placed themselves "voluntarily under the authority of their Church, promising to teach its doctrines and accept its discipline." When the time comes that a clergyman "can no longer conscientiously teach something central to his church's doctrine. . . . which he has solemnly undertaken to teach". . . the only honorable course is resignation. The logic looks impeccable; and perhaps the strategy too has been well thought out. For no doubt the Evangelical Council would argue that the effectiveness of the Church of England during the last decade has been seriously weakened by the Church's excessive tenderness to exponents of "new" theology and morality who have contributed to the sapping of her vitality and integrity.

It would be difficult to refute such reasoning. Certainly some of us tend to prick up our ears whenever we hear Church spokesmen blaming the present weakness of Christian evangelism primarily on to the division of the churches and their failure to unite. All the evidence of the past is that divided churches can evangelize with great zeal and effectiveness. Indeed it may be that the intensity of conviction which makes compromise with separated fellow Christians of other communions difficult, is itself the very quality which issues in fervent evangelism. What has latterly weakened the Church's impact on the world has not primarily been its evident institutional dividedness — regrettable as that dividedness is — but the diluted and uncertain character of its message, the fact that its most basic credal truths could be openly queried, even mocked, by apparently accredited members of its pastoral hierarchy and its supposed intellectual élite. The dilution of the gospel message and the flabbiness of the moral stand against the perversions of the day, these are the factors that have saddened the Church's faithful by disarming them of the instruments of cohesive confrontation with devilry and despair. The symbol of the Church's standing vis-à-vis the unbelieving world is a rock. Eminent ecclesiatics and wayward theologians have got to work upon the rock with the chemistry of dissolution and transformed it into a jelly.

The adherents of supernaturally-grounded authority, whether Evangelical or Catholic, will naturally find common ground against the agents of dissolution. It is notable that in the challenge quoted above from the Evangelical Council to the authors of the aberrant volume the Council did not lay emphasis on the fact that heretics were misrepresenting Holy Writ and undermining the authority of the Scriptures. Instead the Council protested that the heretics were flouting "the authority of their Church" and breaking their promise "to teach its doctrines and accept its discipline." The authority of the Church, the doctrine of the Church, the discipline of the Church—these are marks of the Church's status and significance more commonly associated with the Catholic than with the Evangelical mind. If the true Catholic note is steadfast adherence to the credal doctrines of the Church and unashamed preservation of the Church's authority in this respect, then that is what the Evangelical Council appears to be about in its protest against heresy and ecclesiastical indiscipline.

There is nothing surprising in this merging of Evangelical with Catholic deference to authority under the impact of liberal anarchy. Did not C.S. Lewis foresee the natural coming together of "Low" and "High" Churchmen, indeed of Christians attached to different denominations, by the sheer *depth* of their Christian commitment? He noted that Christians do not come together in sympathy and understanding across denominational barriers by living and thinking on the periphery of their respective communions but by being at the center of their respective communions. Seeking for a word to describe those who refuse to dilute the supernatural basis of the faith, he tentatively proposed the term "deep Christians."

It might be hazardous to attempt to define the "deep Christian" as here conceived. No doubt there would be much to say about his inner spiritual rootedness in God's love, his prayerfulness, his selflessness. But certainly there are two marks of the "deep Christian" that are essential to the rest: his sensitivity to divine Grace and his sensitivity to authority. These two, the determinants of his moral and intellectual course, are balanced aspects of Christian commitment that stem from basic doctrines of man's relationship to God.

For Christianity is different from all other creeds in the doctrine of divine Grace, with its insistence on the divine initiative. God is the worker; we are his tools only. We do not move in our own strength; we are moved by the divine principle — or we are moved by the demonic principle. The truths of faith lift from our shoulders the kind of responsibility laid by other movements on their members, and place a different duty there. The survival of Christianity does not depend on men and women in the same way as, say, the survival of a political party depends on men and women. God is not dependent on our loyal support. The Church will survive — its living past membership renders it already indestructible — whether or not in our age it cuts a pretty figure in the eyes of heaven. This assurance has given to many notable Christians a high-spiritedness, a refusal to take themselves too seriously, which advocates of solemn causes often lack. Their example reminds us that we can try to take too much upon ourselves as Christians; we can try too hard; we can be too ingenious. The images of ourselves as children of a Father and sheep of a Shepherd remain valid.

The Christian life is exacting — but it is exacting primarily in the obedience it demands. The practice of drawing upon spiritual resources outside ourselves, of nourishing ourselves upon a living tradition, of advancing in understanding by disciplined assimilation, is crucial to the Christian pilgrimage and yet runs counter to certain fashionable notions of how you progress in the truth. The communications media encourage us to think differently of progress in knowledge and understanding. They have to, because they are in for the popularity stakes. They are involved in commercial rivalries over maximum ratings for audience or readership. When they enter the world of thought and understanding, they must do so without being exacting, and that is a self-contradictory requirement. So in this sphere the media depend for entertainment on the garnering of conflicting opinions, the provocation of jolly or abrasive interchange, the quick round-up of rival conclusions, and sometimes the final pronouncement of a sort of verdict—often an ambiguous or noncommittal one.

The fact that decisive and useful conclusions are rarely arrived at does not deter the media from inculcating the notion that the harvesting of random, round-the-table contributions, however disparate or ill-informed, is the proper recipe for getting at the truth. The idea seems to be that truth can be accumulated by aggregation rather as money is gathered in at the collection in church. And in some places even the world of education has been corrupted by the notion that healthy intellectual activity is a matter of ceaseless communal ferment, continuing dialogue, endless chitter-chatter in the assertive exchange of ill-pondered opinions. The virtues of silent individual study—patient, assimilative, reflective—have in some quarters been neglected in favor of the process of for-ever gathering together in groups to pool spontaneous conversational throwaways—a process which, as one cynic observed, is neatly designed to cultivate that ignorant articulacy which is the passport to social success. I have myself known students who were anxious only to learn, who had real self-knowledge, genuine humility, love of reading, and a healthy distaste for glib, unreflective chatter in connection with their serious studies. And I have heard such students criticized—even marked down by their tutors—for "not contributing to discussion," when the discussion in question was probably not worth listening to, let alone contributing to, and when the student in question may well have been the only one in the group fully to recognize the unfittedness of each of them to make any worthwhile contribution.

No one would wish to depreciate the value of the informed discussion group in which a number of students who are working on a common topic or a common text come together to share individual insights and to challenge each other where individual interpretation and deduction may seem to have been too glibly and unreflectively arrived at. The practical discipline can be an excellent one. It gives vitality to private study which may otherwise be too limited or remote; it enriches the individual's pursuit with a sense of communal responsibility; and it provides an impulse for further and deeper research. But techniques that lightly give priority to discussion over learning assert a primacy for the individual intuition, spontaneously voiced, that is disquieting. And the idea that truth can be harvested from a range of such variously opinionated offerings is absurd. Moreover it carries the presupposition that the individual is an isolated source of creative, original thought — a presupposition which collides with the Christian ideal of quality as analyzed in the last chapter, and which runs counter to everything we have said about the individual's dependence upon the inheritance of communal tradition for the criteria and machinery of rational thought and for the very substance of his culture.

The Church needs to beware of the infection that renders the frame of secular education so feverishly unstable. It can have no truck with the notion that the communal pooling of ignorance, however articulate, has educative value. The Church has a great intellectual inheritance to hand on. Its members have to learn what that inheritance is. And teaching them what that inheritance is differs sharply from asking them all what they want and what they think it ought to be.

There is something in the very nature of Christianity that resists the recourse to individual opinionatedness. It resists the personal takeover, the human itch for proprietorship, the desire to stamp oneself upon it and to deliver it to the world with a guarantee of personal approbation. Confronted by Christian truth, you are face to face with something that has to be assimilated and grown into, not dressed up presentably for promulgation. One of the weaknesses of aberrant theologians who spill their novel theories over the ecclesiastical scene is that they try too hard. They see themselves as modern men, and they are determined to knock Christianity into shape to meet the exigencies of their time. But Christianity has for two thousand years resisted being knocked into shape to meet the exigencies of any particular age or fashion. Bring your opinionated cleverness to bear upon it, and you will find that it has slipped through your fingers. It was designed for the pure in heart, not for the ingenious in intellect; for babes and sucklings, not for those addicts who turn every objective fact they encounter into a unit for their construct-yourself-a-faith kit. We must all examine ourselves in this respect. Very often what we mean when we say that we want to give Christianity the stamp of our age is that we want to give it our own personal stamp; we want to take it over instead of allowing it to take us over. We have always been tempted to make gods in our own image; increasingly we are tempted to refashion Christ in our own image — and then to award him a testimonial for being so just right.

Kierkegaard constructs an interesting analogy to characterize would-be improvers of Christianity. He notes how a fortune which no rightful inheritors have claimed will, after a period of years, revert to the state to be used as they choose by men without title to it, knowledge of the true proprietor and his intentions having been lost. Liberal theologians treat Christianity in the same way as these men treat the unclaimed fortune. Its true proprietor and master — God — has withdrawn into the shadows and his voice is no longer heard, so the theologians take Christianity over for themselves, assuming proprietorial ownership which entitles them to do exactly what they want with it. They think they have the right to decide "to abolish it altogether, or to modify it *ad libitum*, very much as we might deal with our own possession or invention, treating Christianity, not as something which *in obedient subservience to God's majesty* MUST be believed, but as something which in order to be acceptable must try by the aid of *reasons* to satisfy 'the age,' 'the public'..."

One needs only to read lines like those, from *The Point of View of My Work as an Artist*, written in 1848, published posthumously in 1859, to realize that the faithful Christian's worries do not change much from age to age. Here again is kinship with the past which is one of the Christian's strongest safeguards against error. When the Christian of today reads a sentence like Kierkegaard's, quoted above, he feels at one with an undented tradition at which diluters of the faith in every age have struck in vain. Can he therefore get over-excited about the latest resuscitation of ancient heresy—the latest book doubting Christ's divinity or man's fallen state—as though it even had the bloom of freshness and the spark of new life in it?

Yet heresy is always presented as something "new," for its very invention springs from the itch for change, the lust for novelty, and the urge to denigrate the past. Of course the tendency to praise the latest thing and dispraise the established thing is in fact logically self-contradictory and practically self-defeating. For today is always tomorrow's yesterday. The present is always the future's past. And the principle of discrediting the past in favor of the present commits one to a future of perpetually self-proliferating error.

The lust for novelty is a long-ingrained weakness of human nature. Shakespeare pinpointed it in five of the most shrewdly concentrated lines he ever wrote about human nature in general:

> One touch of nature makes the whole world kin,
> That all with one consent praise new-born gawds,
> Though they are made and moulded of things past,
> And give to dust that is a little gilt
> More laud than gilt o'erdusted.

We rush to praise the "new-born gawds"—the latest things however cheap and spurious. The new rubbish with the gilt surface is valued more than the genuine old gold that has accumulated a coat of dust. This is the touch of nature that binds human beings together in kinship, one aspect of original sin.

Aberrant theology, being rooted in the lust for novelty, bears evident testimony to the power of original sin and therefore finds that doctrine uncomfortable to live with. Heresy has always been with us. If it seems to be riding high at the present time, that is an inevitable concomitant of the decay in deference to authority which is decomposing our civilization generally. But surely there never was a time when heretics were more easily recognizable for what they are. We know the authentic Christian voice—it is the voice of one gripped by the authority of Christianity, who wants it, allows it, to make him what he should be. We know the unmistakable heretical voice—it is the voice of one who grips Christianity by his own authority, to make it what he wants it to be. We are surrounded by "theological" mentors who do not sound in the least like men so imbrued with Christianity, its doctrine, its ethic, its spirituality, its practice, that they overflow with the richness and the assurance of it. We are surrounded by "theological" mentors for whom Christianity has ceased to be a matter of life and death, of conviction and action, and has become a field of speculation. It has ceased to be something you are decisively with or against, and has become a kind of mental plasticine which can be molded into any shape you please in conducting a running commentary on current affairs.

When a heretical academic "theologian" turns to demolish credal doctrine, he does not announce, "I have ceased to believe in Christianity," because in his eyes that would be like picking up a handful of blancmange powder and saying, "I don't like the shape of this blancmange." The blancmange has no shape until the powder is mixed and cooked; and Christianity cannot be believed or disbelieved until the theologian has written his book and given it a shape. He treats the Christian tradition as a religion-powder which the clever modern scholar can mix and cook into something to satisfy personal appetite. His thinking makes the mixture gel, and behold, the finished mold, the real thing, authentic Christianity, now at long last revealed and made available to the human race, turns out to be just that particular collection of views that he has reached at this moment Anno Domini of his changing pilgrimage. He will be the first to admit, however, that his successor in academic office will have to justify his tenure of the post by starting afresh and reaching a quite different conclusion. So "theological" speculators offer us a perpetually self-nullifying "Christianity" of which the only certain thing that can be said is that what it is today it will not be tomorrow.

To whatever instabilities we turn our attention in analysis of the current scene—to the spectacle of aberrant theologians plunging into heresy, to the flight from rationality in the field of education, or the even more tragic departures from sanity at the personal level—we become aware of the remedial necessity for the rehabilitation of the concept of authority in the modern world.

4

Where do we stand against worldliness?

CHRISTIAN BELIEF IS a matter of intellectual, moral, and spiritual commitment. Intellectually, belief involves assent to the interpretation of the human situation contained in the fundamentals of Christian dogma. Morally, belief is commitment to God's purposes for us as revealed through the demands of Church and conscience. (As self-deceiving sinners we naturally like to pretend that these two are frequently in conflict; but probably genuine conflict between the two is rare.) Spiritually, belief is personal rootedness in the eternal order by reference to which "the World" and its ways stand under judgment.

Now it is evident that many Christians reject in some measure the threefold discipline—intellectual, moral, and spiritual—which their Christian profession logically imposes upon them. This rejection presents a threefold difficulty. At the intellectual level, the Church has to deal with theological error and misunderstanding.

At the moral level, the Church has to deal with human pride. At the spiritual level, the Church has to deal with worldliness.

In so far as the Christian rejects any of the three disciplines demanded of him by his Christian profession, to that extent he allies himself with the forces of unbelief. He is baptized, he is perhaps a practicing churchman in that he takes part in certain services, and he calls himself a Christian; but in respect of the threefold demand asserted above he may have largely ceased to believe. Thus he has become, in effect, an unbelieving Christian.

It has been frequently said that the problem of unbelief is the peculiar problem of our age. It must also be admitted that the problem presented by the unbelieving "Christian" is a more taxing one than that presented by unbelieving non-Christians. One expects non-Christians to be unbelievers, and therefore the problem they present to the Church is a clear, unsubtle one. But traditionally Christians have been believers and most Christians (there are some noisy exceptions) still think of themselves as believers—and indeed pass themselves off on the non-Christian world as believers. Thus the problem presented to the Church by unbelieving Christians is a knotty and confused one.

We are not here concerned directly with the fact that many Christians of limited education cannot share deeply in the rich inheritance of thought and art which centuries of Christian culture have handed on to us. This is not a grave problem. When we speak of theological error and misunderstanding, we are thinking of the mental condition of self-styled intellectuals rather than of simple people. We are thinking of those (there are plenty of clergy and "theologians" among them) whose judgment has latterly become clouded by the resurgence of pantheism and humanism masquerading as "Christian." The ignorance or simplicity of the man in the pew is a different matter. It is, in a sense, God-given. And we must not forget this. Indeed it is a source of comfort to remember that the same simplicity (or obtuseness) which sometimes causes the man in the pew to get it all wrong when God's word is sincerely expounded to him probably more often enables him to get it all wrong when heresy is expounded to him. The unlettered man, well-grounded in simple faith by an orthodox upbringing, can sometimes have a built-in resistance to corruption by theological novelty. Hearing from the pulpit what is in effect an insidious attack upon a fundamental doctrine of the faith, he may misunderstand, and the attack misfires. However, the unassuming simplicity which protects some souls from corruption can make others the easy victims of persuasive heretics who stand before them clothed in seeming academic prestige.

But the intention here is not to analyze the character of the theological illiteracy rampant in pulpit and seminary. Rather we must look at the graver and profounder spiritual problem which underlies it: the refusal of many who profess themselves Christians even to try to ground their allegiances in a kingdom which is not of this world. Here is a root cause of the present malaise in the Church — a refusal to choose between God and Mammon — and it is manifested first in a rejection of the notion that godless secularism needs to be redeemed, rejection of the notion that godless secularism is in a fallen condition. In short there are "Christians" among us who no longer speak and behave as though the Fall consists in rejecting God. Rather they act as though the Fall consists in rejecting godless secularism. They would try to "heal" the Church of its anti-secularism. They turn basic Christian doctrines upside down. They propagate a "religionless" Christianity designed to rescue faithful believers from the "pharisaism" and "bigotry" of asserting that man is sinful and needs salvation. This topsy-turvy "Christianity" exudes a mush of undifferentiated sentimentality in the name of omni-indulgent "love." In the face of this "love" it is accounted an outrage to point to human wickedness or hint at damnation. Christianity has been stood on its head. The doctrine of Redemption has been turned inside out. The Love that finds wickedness so powerful that it rescues the desperately lost at the cost of blood and sacrifice has become the "love" that sheds a benign smile of approval on the deeds of sinner and saint alike.

It is important to characterize correctly the new ecumenism which tries to bring together the worshippers of God and the worshippers of Mammon at a common holy and worldly table. We must see it in historic perspective, for the predominant force of worldliness changes from age to age. In the nineteenth century the Church was tempted to the same treachery — but in a different guise. The nineteenth-century treachery, widely succumbed to — as our history and our literature testify—was the desire to give the benediction of Christianity to the "good life" as conceived by prudent money-makers and zealous empire-builders. But commerce and imperialism are alike out of fashion among the leaders of middlebrow thought today. The twentieth–century counterpart of this temptation is the desire to give the benediction of Christianity to the "good life" as conceived by progressive middle-class hedonists. Thus moderate sexual promiscuity, selective homosexuality, skepticism about the supernatural, and comfortable captivation by the mechanical gimmickry of a technological age have to be brought within the orbit of "the Christian." When this is achieved (and a certain powerful force in "theological" journalism is working at full steam to achieve it), the potential conflict between God and Mammon will have been resolved for a whole generation of spiritual layabouts. Non-liturgical intercommunion will give pleasure at board and bed. Religionless worship will rise in sacramental snores from a million centrally-heated flatlets. And canned man, sealed in his automobile, will be wrapped in the paper label coveted for him by the radicals: "New Blend: Holy Worldliness: Guaranteed Christian at No Extra Cost."

One has to keep a clear head in order to characterize this particular drift correctly. The contemporary middle-class "liberal" hedonist, who strives to give a Christian veneer to fundamentally this-worldly values, sometimes poses as a rebel by the specious propaganda that he is up against the established Powers-that-Be in their official bigotry, respectability, and conventionality. But the revolutionary pose deceives no one. For of course bigotry, respectability, and conventionality are now so decisively out of fashion, so generally at a discount, that in so far as there is a pharisaical stronghold in the domain of social attitudes it is precisely represented by middle-class hedonism itself. It is the middle-class hedonist's values which are now imposed by influential voices from television, the daily press, and weekend journalism. In so far as there is a pharisaical stronghold in contemporary English culture (and we appear to have this in common with the rest of the Western world), it is represented by the unargued assumption on the part of this group of the correctness of their own viewpoint. One must not exaggerate, of course, either the numerical strength of this group or the depth of its influence. But its grip on the communications media and its noisiness together erect a fortress of opinion in our midst that is monolithic in self-satisfaction. This body of thought represents one of the noisiest, most persistent, and most identifiable of current attitudes and it certainly cannot be classed as wholly revolutionary. Middle-class hedonism carries the note of today's *Zeitgeist* as surely as imperialism carried the note of the Victorian *Zeitgeist*.

The attempt to dress unregenerate middle-class hedonistic values in borrowed baptismal vesture has, no doubt, in individual cases, personal psychological causes such as cannot possibly concern us here. But is is necessary to be awake to the spiritual problem lying behind this attempt, and to analyze the devices by which the attempt, when articulated, manages to assume a plausible front. Examples are everywhere to hand. I recall a piece of "theological" journalism in which the notion of sin, as orthodoxly understood, was obliquely discredited by sleight of pen. The trick consists in so writing that other people's condemnation of sin or avoidance of sin is made to arouse the emotive antagonism which only sin itself (a very different thing) should properly call out. There are ways of writing — any advertiser or writer can choose to adopt them or not to adopt them — by which a sliding series of slightly false inferences gradually turns the truth upside down. Thus, as in the case of the article recollected here, a person who has spoken out against some sin to condemn it can be made by degrees to appear too much concerned with sin, then too interested in sin, then perhaps fascinated with sin, then indeed "obsessed" with sin, finally altogether too much involved with sin, indeed too sinful. Conversely a conscienceless and shameless person into whose head the notion of sin never enters can be made to appear unconcerned with sin, unconnected with sin, uninterested in sin, uninvolved with sin, unconscious of sin, guileless, innocent, indeed in effect sinless. With a little exploitation of easily loaded terms like "pious" and "devout," gradually sliding into "moralistic" and "legalistic," then into "unforgiving" and "pharisaical," a stand against wickedness can gradually be made to appear wholly inhuman and repellent. Conversely by convenient recourse on the other side to equally emotive terms like "thoughtless" and "impulsive," gradually sliding into "frank" and "spontaneous," then into "sincere" and even "innocent," the life of sin can be made to appear something rather infectiously free of pretence and pretentiousness. Choose your words carefully and this little literary exercise can be exploited to devastating effect. Lay emphasis on the weaknesses of the flesh, evade any hint of the price often paid for them in silent suffering, and you can soon turn values upside down. You can create in your reader's mind a set of emotive attitudes hostile to all firmly married Christians as hypocritical, sin-obsessed prigs, and indulgent to all jolly unbelieving fornicators and smooth adulterers as guileless, frank, unassuming dispensers of sympathy and happiness to their charmingly unfrigid fellow creatures.

Nothing is easier than writing in which talk about sin is steamrollered by talk about compassion. But let us not be blinded as we read. For *talk* about compassion is no more compassion than *talk* about sin is sin. Journalism is one thing, and life is another and (thank God) very different thing. Somehow it seems to happen, unless my experience is oddly untypical, that those priests who speak most urgently of sin also deal most gently with their erring brothers and sisters and spend themselves most costingly for the sinners they are called to minister to. Indeed one may question whether deep compassion for the sinner can possibly exist without a correspondingly fierce hatred of the sins which disfigure him. This is a general principle of human relationships. The teacher is not offended by bad work from a pupil of whom he has a poor opinion as he is offended by bad work from a favorite pupil whose talents he admires.

It is of course a matter of simple logic that the Church, in so far as She condemns sin plainly and firmly, to that extent can extend the maximum sympathy, compassion, and unquestioning acceptance to the sinner without the slightest possibility of misunderstanding or betrayal. Only in so far as the Church clearly identifies what is sinful can She open her arms to all sinners. Clear identification and condemnation of sin is the very precondition of mercy and forgiveness. Without this identification and condemnation, mercy is vulgarized into indulgence and forgiveness is perverted into apathetic lack of interest. What is the value of forgiveness if there is nothing to forgive? What is the cost of mercy where sins are reckoned of no account? What is the quality of compassion so smooth that it flows untroubled by detestation of wickedness?

The kind of thinking here exemplified represents only one of a thousand devices exploited by the exponents of hedonism for propaganda purposes. Basically, the emotive appeal derives its force from selected false antitheses. The particular antitheses in question imply contradiction between attitudes that are in reality not mutually opposed. A contradiction is implied between compassion for sinners and clear recognition of sin as sin, when in fact the most compassionate man is likely to be the man most sensitive to the character of evil. A contradiction is implied between forgiveness of sinners and clear condemnation of sin when again, in practice, the two are linked in mutual corroboration. So it goes on. A contradiction is implied between sympathy for sinners and sensitivity to their wickedness, between the virtue of charity and lucid moral analysis, between the assertion of binding moral standards and the Christian virtue of humility. The confusion is then more deeply confounded by subtly compounding the devices that insidiously ally sympathetic emotions with condonation of evil, and forbidding rigidity with defense of good. By easy transitions, hypocrisy, priggishness, self-righteousness, and pharisaism are mixed up in a messy verbal hash along with piety, devoutness, orthodoxy, and attendance at public worship; while sincerity, humility, frankness, and unassumingness are baked in a solid verbal pie along with fornication, homosexuality, skepticism, and undisciplined religionlessness. The implicit contradictions are totally unreal. The hash and the pie are alike compounded of ingredients not only incongruous but mutually repellent.

The effectiveness of these devices lies in setting the head of the impressionable Christian in a spin. He knows the Christian call for lovingkindness, compassion, tenderness, and forgiveness; he is made to question whether he is not failing in these virtues by denying a Christian blessing to all manner of adulterous and illicit relationships. The trick consists in focusing attention on the (admittedly often genuine) unhappinesses and frustrations of men and women with tangled sex lives, and then turning a proper request for compassion in dealing with particular cases into a general prescription of Christian benediction upon all varieties of vice. A curtain is conveniently drawn over the lot of forsaken partners and abandoned children. No one who has worked in higher education and been repeatedly confronted by the maturing offspring of broken homes can possibly be fooled by the drawing of this curtain. The pattern repeats itself with monotonous regularity. Find an unhappy student, an unstable student, a student wracked by secret worries, agonized by unnameable apprehensions, troubled about himself or herself, deeply in need, sometimes tragically in need of support, security, and comfort that are not being found; and in nine cases out of ten there is parental divorce, infidelity, separation, or other domestic disturbance in the background. The man who has spent a few hours with the wracked and tormented young people who pay the price of parental liberation, and then goes home to pick up a Church journal or a theological book in which "Christian" blessings are being poured on the agents of disaster in a tone oozing with pseudo-pious sentimentality, is apt to break out in a fury of denunciation. It is one of the biggest lies by which the Devil deceives our generation to pretend that the man of true compassion will back the loosening of moral and domestic ties out of tenderness to adults whose sexual selfishness and wantonness has landed them in a mess. The man of true compassion will recall the unseen faces of the betrayed and the abandoned, young and old, and in the name of that compassion press for the kind of institutional rigor that reinforces conscience and responsibility instead of the kind of institutional flabbiness that condones and indulges selfish appetites.

We must not talk as though it were only (or indeed primarily) in respect of sexual *mores* that dangerous alliances between the Church and the World are made. The ecumenical campaign for reunion between Christians and Mammonites has other faces. We may consider a fashionable vein of thought which may be roughly represented by such statements as the following: "The Church must follow her Lord and devote herself in service to the world he came to save. The Church, like our Lord, must not seek to rule the world but to serve the world. The Church in the past has tried to be the world's master; it has to learn to be the world's servant. It has to kneel and wash the world's feet."

Statements of this kind are of course unexceptional if their context is right and if the implications which they are made to carry are sound. But every educated Christian knows that the words "world" and "World" are used with diverse connotations in the New Testament and in Christian literature. As long as such statements carry the meaning that it is the Christian's duty to serve the needs of others, in however humble a capacity, they can do no harm. But when such statements are made to carry the meaning (or convey the innuendo) that the Christian's duty is to subordinate his Christian valuations, criteria, judgments, or doctrines to secularism's valuations, criteria, judgments, or doctrines, then the statements are false and dangerous. At the theoretical level, the Church's judgment upon secularism is decisive and irrevocable. Secularism, the godless culture, is lost. It is "this World" whose Prince is judged. Since the essential function of the Church is to desecularize the secular by Christianizing it, the antithesis between Christianity and secularism is irreconcileable. At the practical level, the Christian's duty is to serve all, bringing help, sympathy, and charity to fellow Christians and non-Christians alike. But this practical activity of non-differentiation between Christians and others in the giving of help, sympathy, charity, and by whatever talent or temperament one has to give, will be open, frank, and free of misunderstanding only in so far as the general judgment upon secularism is clearly and decisively articulated. The case here is exactly parallel to the case we have already made in respect of the false antithesis between condemnation of sin and compassion for sinners. Once more, clarity and firmness at the theoretical universal level make possible the maximum compassion and sympathy at the practical particular level. Only in so far as the Church makes clear its overall judgment upon secularism as such can the individual Christian readily and without misunderstanding involve himself wholeheartedly in serving the needs of the world wherever the personal demand confronts him.

There is no doubt that at present professedly Christian voices keep urging us to serve the world as a Christian duty when what in fact they are inviting us to do is to form the kind of alliance between Church and secularism which would be treachery to our Lord. It is not the Church's business to blur the distinction between a godless civilization and the kingdom of God. It is certainly the

Christian's duty to enter into the life of that civilization in the form of a servant; but in so far as he enters effectively, to that extent the civilization ceases to be a secular civilization at the point of his entry. That is to say, the Christian enters into the world's affairs directed by the will of God and carried along by the grace of God. Thus, as he enters the world's affairs, through no virtue of his own, the divine Will which directs him and the divine Grace that carries him make their entry into those affairs within and through him. This represents, on however minute a scale, a movement of desecularization. The Christian, in so far as he moves and acts Christianly, to that extent desecularizes all he touches. He cannot help doing so. Or rather he cannot help being the vehicle by which God does so; for that is what being a Christian amounts to.

The kind of illogicality which undermines Christianity by pressing the call to Christians to serve the world in preference to "serving the Church" as such—that is, to be involved in social activities to the neglect of specifically religious duties—reaches its climactic extreme in a misleading claim. The claim is that "Christ's way is the way of self-sacrifice. He died in order to rise again. The Church too must sacrifice itself; it must die in order to live afresh." Now though there is substance in this if it is interpreted at the personal level as an exhortation to individual Christians to spare no cost in walking in Christ's way, it is plainly nonsensical if it is regarded as an invitation to the Church as an institution to annihilate itself or even to mute its specifically ecclesiastical claims. The Church as an institution must keep alive the call to Christian self-sacrifice. If the Church "dies," then the call is silenced. If a headmaster were in the habit of quieting his assembled school for prayer by calling loudly for "Silence," it would be absurd to claim that his noisy proclamation of the word was a contradiction of the demand for quiet, and that he ought to act in conformity with his belief in the need for silence by himself setting the right example and shutting up. If he accepted such advice, then you would arrive at the absurdity of all silence being lost because the call to silence was silenced. Just so. You will not spread self-sacrifice in the world by requesting the institution that calls for self-sacrifice to sacrifice itself *qua* institution.

Too much sloppy thinking and speaking has gathered round the confusion between the universal and the particular, between what it is proper to prescribe for a body and what it is proper to prescribe for an individual member of that body. If moral advice appropriate to the individual were applied to the body of which he is a member *in toto* as though it were an individual with a mind and will of its own, you would arrive at absurd contradictions. Even in sport we talk about individuals sacrificing themselves for the team, not about teams sacrificing themselves. If the Church as a body were what it is assumed to be by those who prescribe self-sacrifice for it as though it could have a moral life that matched those of its members, then it would be absurd, for instance, to give money to the Church. You would be virtually giving it to yourself; and the Church's duty would be unselfishly to refuse it.

We have to contend with the difference between the universal and the particular whenever we have recourse to generalizations about "Christianity" and "secularism" for the reasons we have already referred to. There is a sense in which the Christian cannot live in a secular society because in so far as he lives in it it is not secular. At the point of his conscious Christian involvement in it, it is no longer a secular society. Of course the requisite involvement must be consciously Christian, an involvement under the direction of a will given over in obedience to God, of a spirit grounded in his kingdom, of a mind alert to the Christian interpretation of life's meaning and purpose. In short it must be the involvement of a believer as already defined—of a Christian accepting the threefold disciplines, intellectual, moral, and spiritual, demanded of him by his Christian profession.

These disciplines are what save the involved Christian from becoming a treacherous Christian. They enable him to come fully into the world without becoming of the World; they allow him to act fruitfully among secularists without degenerating into a temporizer. Any notion that this protective armor of the intellectual, moral, and spiritual disciplines is no longer needed in the modern "educated" world—any notion that the Christian has nothing to defend but only something to share—should have been dispelled by the difficulties and confusions of the last two decades. It is now clear to the thoughtful that the hope of converting the world by the device of labelling it "Christian" in advance of conversion has not been justified by results.

It will be appropriate now to underline and amplify a point made earlier. Those Christians, in any age, who try to accommodate worldliness by diluting the Christian demand are essentially of a single mental breed, even though superficially they may appear to be very different in their thinking. This is because, as has already been said, the predominant character of worldliness changes from age to age. Those nineteenth and early twentieth century Christians who sought to accommodate prevailing worldliness by giving the "Christian" label to imperialism, nationalism, and the class-bound society, are succeeded in the later twentieth century by Christians who seek to accommodate the prevailing worldliness by giving the "Christian" label to hedonism, promiscuity, and our mechanized house-bound culture. The latter are the direct heirs of the former. Those for whom Christianity was synonymous with keeping the rich man secure in his castle and the poor man at his gate, with painting the world map imperial red and ruling the inferior races firmly from above, those in whose eyes God made England mighty and would make her mightier yet — they were the immediate direct ancestors of those today for whom Christianity is synonymous with keeping the liberal humanist, the hedonist, and the affluence-addict morally comfortable in their skepticism and their self-indulgence.

Thus many so-called "radical" theologians are paradoxically among the great reactionaries of our age, the arch-opponents from within of the rebellious Church. They reject the essentially revolutionary character of Christianity by virtue of which it is always in conflict with the prevailing worldly ethos of the age. They want to turn Christianity into the great corroborative spiritual buttress of our culture's current materialistic ethos. Of course they and their followers do not see themselves thus, because they have failed to discern that shift in the predominant character of worldliness which calls for a Christian emphasis appropriate to the condition of the modern world and the biases of the modern mind. This failure of a vociferous group allegedly devoted to liberation and progress to reckon with the inner character of the modern mind is not in itself surprising. Historically speaking, it was to be expected. Rebels against Christian orthodoxy are always reactionary because orthodoxy is essentially revolutionary. Rebels against Christian orthodoxy are always out of date because orthodoxy is always, by its very character, at war with prevailing worldliness and not with the worldliness of a previous generation.

In this case the failure of liberational radicalism to answer the need of the age has produced a situation of unusual confusion and tension because the shift in character from nineteenth-century worldliness to twentieth-century worldliness has been such a sharp one. For this reason, the parallel shift of those within the Church who would try to accommodate Christianity to contemporary worldliness has had to be correspondingly sharp. Nineteenth-century worldliness, by its emphasis on power, suppression, empire-building, and money-making, and by its entanglement with militarism, trade, and the rigors of adventure, was an essentially masculine worldliness. Twentieth-century worldliness, by its emphasis on the home, on the enjoyments and pursuits of pacific affluence, and on the libertarianism and indulgences being won from technological conquest of toil, from medical control of ovulation, and from educational elimination of social crudities, is an altogether less rough, less rigorous, less assertive brand of worldliness. Indeed, deeply entangled as it is in the emotional and sexual-domestic nature of man, it has by contrast with nineteenth-century worldliness a decisively feminine orientation.

The terms "masculine" and "feminine" are used here as convenient conceptual pegs in an attempt to gather together predominant aspects of nineteenth-century and twentieth-century worldliness in separate clusters and identify a civilizational shift. It goes without saying that the Christian is antagonistic to current worldliness whatever its prevalent character may be, and censure of current trends implies no sympathy for past trends. Thus, though a good deal might be said in development of the thesis that our public mind, even in its impress upon the Church, represents an imbalance distinguishable in quasi-sexual terms from the imbalance of a century ago, that would not imply any preference for yesterday's extremes over today's extremes. No thinker, however, can escape the native bias that allies him instinctively with the spirit of his age; he has to make a special effort to identify it and to counter it in himself and in others.

In considering the character of contemporary worldliness as reflected in the literature of the age and the changes made in social life and popular attitudes, one notes the tendency to reject the objective and the authoritative in favor of the subjective and the spontaneous, to reject the rational and the intellectual in favor of the emotional and the intuitive, and to reject the traditional and the institutional in favor of the personal and the capricious. These tendencies, as features of contemporary aberrance, have inevitably become recurring themes in this book. They confront us under varying disguises when we turn to defend Christian doctrine and discipline, Christian institutionalism and practice. We shall come face to face with the issue again when we turn in the final chapter to the Christian's interest in the defense of reason. For subjectivity and the cult of spontaneity challenge the values of truth, order, and stability in which both Christianity and just civilization have a vested interest.

There is, of course, nothing new in pinpointing subjectivity as a disease of our age, and perhaps it is worthwhile to corroborate this point by a specific example. One of my professional interests as a literary man has been the work of James Joyce, whose *Ulysses* may justly be called the major epic work of twentieth century literature. When Joyce was at work on *Finnegans Wake*, the successor to *Ulysses*, a group of his disciples, headed by Samuel Beckett, produced a collection of essays in defense and elucidation of the new work in progress. The essays were published in 1929 under the title, *Our Examination Round His Factification For Incamination Of Work In Progress*. It is pertinent to mention that, since the publication of Joyce's Letters, we now know that Joyce was himself behind the writers of these essays. ("I did stand behind those 12 Marshals more or less directing what lines of research to follow.")

One essay, by Thomas McGreevy, is called "The Catholic Element in Work in Progress." In it McGreevy turns aside for a time from considering *Finnegans Wake* to make some observations about *Ulysses*. Two points he makes have a bearing on our theme. Firstly, he praises Joyce's powers of artistic organization. *Ulysses* reveals "a power to construct on a scale scarcely equalled in English literature since the Renaissance, not even by the author of *Paradise*

Lost." Secondly, he sums up the significance of the book by reference to parallel epics of the past: "For *Ulysses* is an inferno. As Homer sent his Ulysses wandering through an inferno of Greek mythology so Dante himself voyaged through the inferno of mediaeval Christian imagination and so Mr. Joyce sent his hero through the inferno of modern subjectivity."

If there have been times when I felt that in David Martin's use of the expression "massive objectivity" lay the key to half of what I wanted to say in this book, there have also been times when I have felt that in McGreevy's phrase, "the inferno of modern subjectivity" lay the key to the other half of what I wanted to say. That Joyce, one of the greatest writers of the age, should have assaulted its spirit head-on, firstly by fashioning the most finely organized, the most structurally interrelated, the most objectively complex verbal masterpiece of all time, and secondly by making it a voyage through "the inferno of modern subjectivity" strikes me as a notable commentary on the thesis of this book which, by the very nature of its analysis, also has to conduct the reader through the inferno of modern subjectivity. Joyce's realization of how the twentieth century Everyman (such is Leopold Bloom, the Dublin Jew) would try in his dreams of bliss to fashion mentally a mock-up, materialistic "New Bloomusalem," a heaven of technologized gimmickry, is remarkably prophetic. His simultaneous endowment of Bloom with a pseudo-religion of cerebrally sentimentalized "Love" (such as we have already touched upon in this chapter) is a further instance of unerring prescience. The twentieth-century Everyman is happy in his inferno, unlike Joyce's alter ego, the artist and lapsed Catholic, Stephen Dedalus. McGreevy pinpoints the contrast, speaking of "this inferno from which Stephen is ever trying spiritually to escape, for he, unlike Jewish Bloom, knows the distinction between the law of nature and the law of grace and is in revolt against the former however unable he be to realize the latter . . . ." I am tempted to quote John Donne: "Is not that too literally, too exactly, thy case?" Is not that a penetrating diagnosis of our condition today — lots of us happy in our inferno, and the rest of us half-heartedly trying to escape, sensing perhaps the distinction between the law of nature and the law of grace, revolting in conscience against the former, but too weak in faith to realize the latter?

The interests and comforts of modern life so obsess us and possess us that our Christian allegiance to a kingdom that is not of this world is forgotten. There is so much in daily experience to corroborate the claims of the world upon us that the call to other-worldliness goes by default. And we are constantly playing down the great objectivities which would protect us from this danger. For instance, long ago the Church in her wisdom established a calendar distinct from the world's calendar. By observing it men could be kept weekly, even daily, aware of the pattern of a way which is not the world's way. By means of the annual cycle, men could live through a reenactment of the Christian story from Creation to Ascension: and of course the Mass itself constitutes a reenactment of the divine sacrifice. It must be accepted, of course, that the showing forth of the Christian reality in word and sacrament and the concretizing of human response in ritual and symbol can of themselves become corrupted when forms and acts are degutted of living human substance. But we are in no danger today of so objectifying our faith and worship as to become mere performers of ceremonies and fulfillers of symbolic duties. Rather our danger is that we shall so internalize our religion as to leave it high and dry on an island of subjectivity over whose shores the waves of real life never lap. For what we fail to recognize is that you cannot make religion live by plunging among living people and promptly for-getting all about it. If Christians do not make worship, prayer, and religious duties important, no one else will even recognize that such things can be. Too many Christians have now got the extraordi-nary idea that if they give themselves up to good works in lieu of religious observances, then grateful people all around them will be mystically infected with some vague virus of spirituality and the hand of God will be seen at work. It won't. The Church has got to be seen to be the Church, not only in the interests of those we would convert — whose souls can never be saved by a voluntary social welfare agency, however caring — but also in the interests of Christians themselves, whom God has made in such a way that they cannot possibly nourish a faith *in vacuo*.

Behind all this lies a simple error. Many Christians have been deceived into believing that what cuts them off from others outside the Church is bad. They have been tricked into playing down as socially or emotionally divisive the beliefs and practices that set them apart. In so doing they cut away the ground from under their own feet. We took the Church's calendar as an example. The Church's calendar is a good thing, not *in spite of* the fact that it is different from the world's calendar, but *precisely because* it is different from the world's calendar. That is to say, the Church's calendar will not allow us to forget an allegiance which people outside the Church do not recognize. If Christians generally begin to fall for the deceptive fallacy that being Christian essentially means being *with* everybody around them in mind and spirit, then their faith will evaporate. It cannot survive without the embodiment of act and word; and the embodiment of act and word is not just a matter of good works. As we have already shown, good works alone can never distinguish the Christian *qua* Christian. The embodiment of faith in act and word is a matter first of all for the worshipping and evangelizing body—the Church.

One of the massive objectivities under threat from modern subjectivity is the priesthood. The controversy about ordaining women to the priesthood is only one aspect of the threat. It will be agreed that the mystique of the priesthood is closely related to its exclusiveness, that is to say, the way it is hedged about by such restrictions as celibacy and masculinity, and by regulations and ceremonies governing admission to holy orders. In so far as all these disciplines and restrictions set the priesthood apart, they minister to the preservation of one more objective reality embodying the distinctiveness of an institution rooted in the supernatural. To destroy the distinctiveness of an institution rooted in the supernatural is of course to desupernaturalize it. To use worldly notions of egalitarian non-differentiation in order to protest against demarcations which set the things of God apart from the things of Mammon is to play Mammon's game.

Now this is not to deny that there might be a Christianly informed dispute about whether women should be ordained, for an order is not necessarily any the less distinctive, less set apart, because it is open to both sexes, as is evidenced by our mixed medical profession. But what in fact confronts us is so often not a Christianly informed case for or against the ordination of women, but a secularly-grounded argument for ordaining them and an inadequately informed Christian instinct that is vaguely against it.

The controversy is bedevilled by a peculiar modern blindness in respect of the relationship between differentiation of function and differentiation of status. We seem to be losing the sense of differentiations of function which exist outside of and alongside hierarchical gradings and are by no means to be confused with them. Exclusion does not always imply superiority and inferiority. The fact that I am not allowed to direct traffic at a crossroads has never made me feel inferior to the local policeman. The fact that the policeman is not allowed to collect the mail from the post box does not make him feel inferior to the postman. We must not confuse unrelated kinds of authority. The overall authority of the abbess in a medieval priory took happily under its wing the priestly authority of the chaplain, her subordinate, who looked after the community's spiritual life. The authority of a headmistress in a boarding school extends over her Religious Studies department even though one of the staff may be an ordained priest. The authority of the priest is not a rung on the same ladder which gives the headmistress authority over him. The idea that holy orders confer a status in relation to which all laymen are inferior is ridiculous. If traditional orthodoxy denies something to women by restricting the priesthood to men, it is not a superior status of any kind.

The idea of differences that exist aside from all gradations of status seems to be foreign to popular thinking just now. The vulgar use of the word "discrimination" is a case in point. The neutral use of the word "discriminate" (to observe and make careful note of the differences distinguishing things) is falling into desuetude. The verb is being used pejoratively of making invidious distinctions. The idea of *pure* discrimination without placement on a higher or a lower plane is being lost to us. Thus if one has any doubts at all about whether women should be ordained, one is assumed to believe that women are not just different from men, but inferior to men. Our inability to think of human categories without classification into superior and inferior suggests that we must be the most class-obsessed age in all history.

But the priesthood is not something you are equal to by virtue of general human superiority. It is certainly not something you are equal to by virtue of supposed masculine qualities of dynamism, thrust, and leadership. Indeed, far from requiring the exercise of what we now call "personality," the priesthood requires, in a sense, the suppression of personality; it demands depersonalization of the individual, submergence within the office, loss of identity within the role of sacrificing *persona*, vicariously operative on behalf of universal, bi-sexual man.

No doubt traditionalists would argue that woman is less fitted than man for the exercise of such a depersonalized symbolic function. There is the evidence of linguistic usage that the masculine can contain and represent the feminine, and not *vice versa*. Perhaps the bi-sexual connotative coverage of "man," "he," "his" and so on, is not a bare linguistic convention alone but an expression of some deep-seated human awareness like the myth of Eve's creation from Adam's rib. It is not within the scope of this book to go fully into so profound and complex a matter. Our concern is with a wider and more generalized issue. The entanglement of the demand for feminine priesthood with current egalitarian clamor has confused this issue by bringing it within the orbit of the Progressive Emancipation myth that is to be touched upon in the next chapter. As a result, the issue is being falsely simplified into a question of opening a door hitherto closed to women, with the aim of enabling them to do exactly what men at present do. And there is a fallacy here.

The fallacy is that the controversy is really about granting women the right to an identical share in a privilege already open to men — and therefore about effecting a parallel social development to that which gave women votes. Before women had votes they lacked something that men had; after women had won votes they partook fully and exactly of what formerly only men enjoyed. The controversy that led up to the change centered thus not upon the nature of votes but upon the nature (the rights) of women. No one saw the concept of the vote under threat, but the campaign fought fiercely for the concept of womanhood. Now if the right to be ordained is seen in parallel with such a development, the demand for extending the privilege of ordination to women is subsumed within the dynamic of the century's leap forward toward universal political equality of citizenship. And it is treated as essentially a controversy about womanhood, not about priesthood. No one is examining whether a priesthood available to women as well as to men will be a *different* thing in itself from a priesthood only open to men. Indeed the whole basis of the campaign presupposes that exactly what men have is being denied to women. This is what gives the campaign its emotional impetus. The demand for feminine priesthood is, however, so entangled with other asexual demands for undifferentiated participation that it cannot be treated in isolation from them as another step in the lifting of restrictions upon women. Indeed the demand for feminine priesthood is involved with current egalitarian clamor to such an extent that, paradoxically, the latter seems likely in effect to cancel the former out. For the egalitarian impulse which fuels the campaign for women priests at the same time fuels a wider campaign for opening up the functions of the priestly office to more of the laity. In short, women are pressing for ordination for their sex simultaneously with the growth of another notion challenging more widely the exclusiveness of the present all-male priesthood, the notion that there is something undemocratic about the restriction of certain practices to the priesthood.

Not long ago an article appeared in the London *Times* by a layman pleading for fuller use of the laity in the work and worship of the Church, and there was a good deal of sense in this plea. However, speaking apparently as a Lay Reader, he seemed to regret that Lay Readers are "more or less confined to the taking of evensong," not a well-attended service at a time when "the prevailing fashion" is for family Communion. Clearly the writer wanted Lay Readers to be able to officiate at the sacrament. "If, for the present (*sic*), we confine the celebration of the Eucharist to the 'officer class' of the clergy...." the argument ran, implying some sort of parallel between the privilege of standing at the altar, celebrating the Eucharist, and the possession of a commission in the army.

This article corroborates our point. Laywomen are not the only people hungry for priestly office or function. Moreover the article draws a vague parallel between the priesthood and privileges like that of using the Officers' Mess which are denied to other ranks. In so doing it (intentionally, I assume) misconceives the character of the priesthood in order to hint that there is something too rigidly hierarchical about it. This article is representative of a growing current of opinion. A bishop has recently been asking in the press, Why should not Church Army captains be allowed to celebrate Holy Communion? It is surely a small step from this to asking why Churchwardens or Sunday school teachers should not be allowed to celebrate Holy Communion.

Without wishing to be irreverent, one would wish at this point to draw attention to an observed law of life which has nothing to do with theology or religion specifically, but which common sense will concede to be valid. The law lays down that there are certain desirable things which, the more you open them up in ready accessibility, the more they cease to be. An obvious example is the peaceful countryside made readily accessible by the development of automobile transportation. Those of us who were young in the 1920s and 1930s and were lucky enough to have parents with cars can recall meandering about main roads at twenty or thirty miles an hour, a speed at which even the driver could point to a rabbit in a field for the benefit of his children in the back seat. One could picnic in peace and tranquility on the grass verge at the side of the main road, so rare were the passing vehicles. As a resident now in the Lake District, a tourist area, I am deeply conscious of this natural law whose operation can here be observed at first hand. Those of us who, forty years ago, could pull up a car at the lakeside by Bowness pier, driving down to the water's edge, who could climb out of the car at the head of Kirkstone Pass in the height of summer and breathe the unbroken stillness and calm, cannot seriously pretend that today's trippers have at last won through to what we enjoyed.

There is no intention here to deplore the fact that more people have cars. The intention is to establish a certain principle, namely, that by making a good thing more generally accessible *you may alter the character of the good thing* to such an extent that what is gained by those newly admitted to its enjoyment is not at all what was once available to the restricted few. In short, it is not just the lives of thousands of people that have been transformed by opening up the countryside to them and equipping them with cars. The countryside itself has been transformed. What the many enjoy is *not* what the few enjoyed—and hoped others would increasingly share in.

This analogy from an area of experience far away from the

matter in question will perhaps allow us to approach the burning issue coolly. A bishop, we said, has been asking that Church Army captains should be permitted to celebrate Holy Communion. A Lay Reader has been lamenting that Readers are not permitted (*at present*) to celebrate Holy Communion. The campaign to ordain women is only part of a wider movement toward universal participation in anything and everything without respect to regulated distinction of office or function. And (this is a practical observation, not an argument from principle) it seems likely that the general development pressing for derestriction of priestly functions will move at about the same pace as the movement for ordaining women. Women priests will not be common before a dozen parallel developments have combined to derestrict and, in that sense, devalue the priesthood. Liberal-minded women are doomed by natural law never to get what they want.

The purpose of this argument is to give a new twist to the current controversy. Because the priesthood, as we have understood it, will be destroyed by the admission of women and by parallel developments which the campaign for women priests will accelerate, the fact ought to be faced that the pressing current issue is the abolition of the priesthood as we have understood it, *not* the admission of women to exactly that which men have previously enjoyed. Talk of women priests therefore is as unreal in practical terms as it is self-contradictory to the ecclesiastical rigorist in semantic terms. The real question at issue is whether the time has come for a different kind of ministry, one from which the old restrictive exclusiveness has gone. Any other line of argument is sheer self-deception. If we honestly faced this real practical question, hidden behind the campaign to ordain women, we should then be able to get to grips with the basic impulse which has energized the campaign. And we should probably find that impulse riddled through with secularist presuppositions about status and equality that have no application to the Christian ministry.

5

Where do we stand against current idolatries?

CONSIDERATION OF THE controversy about ordaining women has deflected us from the main course of the argument, but it occupies so many minds feverishly and even painfully at the present time that it would have seemed evasive to ignore it. Precisely because the campaign for ordaining women is at least in part fueled by a dubious "Christian" alliance with current secularist pressures for dissolution of restrictions and erasure of demarcations the issue has its bearing on the central concern of this book. That concern is the analysis of the current interpenetration of Christianity and secularism and of the Christian's need to find the right footing in this situation. The controversy about ordaining women has particular relevance to the concern of the last chapter and the present one — the peculiar kind of worldliness currently in vogue and the conscious Christian disciplines needed to combat it both within the Church and outside it.

The Christian's intellectual, moral, and spiritual disciplines are his only means to stability in the morass of current irrationality, amorality, and materialism. The bases of differentiated Christian commitment are essential footholds at a time when the flood of secularist propaganda would wash away the landmarks of supernaturally-orientated allegiance. The tide muddies even the springs of language. Our words are taken over, smeared with secularist overtones, and returned to us almost too soiled for Christian use. We have seen how this has happened with words like "love," "compassion," and "forgiveness," which have been so freely exchanged as counters in marketing cheap self-indulgence and easy lust that they come back into our hands coated with the grease of a thousand grubby fingers, and are scarcely recognizable as coinage. The King's image is covered with dirt. We wonder whether we dare try to pass the coins off in Christian discourse as valid currency fit to be tendered in the name of the now invisible royal head.

The more you concentrate on the things that make Christianity Christian — and not merely altruistic and humanitarian — the more you become conscious of this process of verbal devaluation. The very words we use for defining our fundamental Christian position may be picked up by secularists, wrung dry of vitality, and then handed back to us with all the rich connotative sap squeezed out of them. We recite "I believe in God" and we intend something decisively binding by the verb "believe." But I once saw a newspaper headline which ran, "75% of the population still believe in God," and the article below turned out to record the findings of an opinion poll in which people had been asked, "Do you believe in God?" No doubt lots of honest people had furrowed their brows momentarily on their doorsteps and had finally decided that they *did* think there was a God at the back of things. But that is a very different thing from believing in God in the sense assumed in the creed. What we affirm is something much more than that we think a God exists. In a life of Christian belief there are at least three major constituents — worship, service, and proclamation — that give body to belief. The believer *worships* God, and worship is something more than religious ceremonies or private prayers; it is also a matter of what you give your heart to as the center and pivot of your world. The believer *serves* God, and service is something more than professing allegiance; it is a matter of what are your ultimate ends in the way you occupy yourself. The believer *proclaims* God, and proclamation is something more than labelling yourself with a denomination when you fill up a form; it is a matter of what you are continually forwarding, or advertising, by the sort of things you do and talk about. For the Christian, belief is a matter of basic mental orientation, overall purpose, and daily behavior and conversation.

Now, accepting this as a Christian account of "belief," what about the man who says, "Oh yes, I believe in God," when his mental orientation, his overall purposes, and his conversational obsessions reveal that in fact he believes primarily and earnestly in the ladder of promotion, the achievement of the maximum number of personal comforts, and the promiscuous pursuit of the opposite sex? Surely he is guilty of a lie if he pretends that he believes in God, when he really believes in promotion, comfort, and sex. Conversely, what about the man who says, "No, I don't believe in any God," when his mental orientation, his daily activity, and his daily chatter reveal that he believes passionately and profoundly in money, cars, and betting on horses? Surely he too is guilty of lying. His gods are money, cars, and gambling. To call the one man a believer (a theist) and the other an unbeliever (an atheist) would be most misleading when one believes in promotion, comfort, and sex, and the other believes in money, cars, and gambling. For practical purposes they are both polytheists. In this sense, it is not atheism and not skepticism, but polytheism, that is endemic in our day. The question that should be asked by the pollster on the doorstep is not "Do you believe in God?" but "Which God or gods do you believe in?"

We live in what is, in effect, a polytheistic society in that we give ourselves, with varying degrees of what can only be called idolatry, to the service of money-making, career-making, power-grabbing, food, drink, fashion, entertainment, cars, gambling, sex, and so on. This assertion does not imply that no man can give attention to these things without guilt. There is a due degree of attention that such things merit. But in fact they are getting excessive attention.

As objects of concern they are attracting the kind and degree of human response more proper to the religious sphere. They have become objects of devotion. As such, they are not any the less divinities in practice because we still print the nouns with small initial letters. People of supposedly darker ages might have had the honesty to endow them with capital letters, to personalize them, to build them temples in their streets as well as altars in their hearts. But it is not capital letters that confer divinity; it is human worship, service, and proclamation that attest godhead—being made the object of the human heart's adoration, the motivating force of the human will's most strenuous efforts, being eulogized by the human tongue as desirable, worth cherishing, and worth sacrifice.

The argument here is that in many respects ours is not a skeptical age so much as a superstitious age. This statement is based not only on the widespread growth of cults like those of the Moonites and the Scientologists, but on the switching of human veneration toward a thousand new idols. The cults are superstitions consciously chosen—even if the choice is irrational and made under mental duress. The idolatries are superstitions slid into by accident—the accident of making some human or material agency the pole star of mental orientation, of guiding purpose and incessant concern. This is called an "accident" in that the human or material agency is genuinely deserving of human attention or respect (as the cults are not), and the slide into that excess which involves servitude to it is not humanly foreseen.

Alcohol is a case in point. I have before me the immediate pre-Christmas edition of a Sunday Newspaper Color Supplement. It consists of forty-eight pages. Thirteen of those pages are devoted to glorifying the consumption of wines and spirits—eleven-and-a-half pages overtly by advertisement, and one-and-a-half pages indirectly through a famous novelist's advice for the avoidance and treatment of hangovers. The novelist obliges by making my point for me:

> Like the search for God, with which it has other things in common, the search for the infallible and instantaneous hangover cure will never be done...... Some sound work has been done on hangover avoidance. (Hangover evasion, in other

words not drinking much or even at all, is unworthy to be discussed in a reputable journal.)

I am not a teetotaller; I like my glass of wine. But with knowledge of human wrecks about me, I find it difficult to share this writer's sense of humor. His article accompanies a series of advertisements in which the consumption of wine and spirits (yes, "the Christmas spirit" is mentioned in one of them) is set by lavish artistry in the context of luxurious living with glamorous companions (all looking sober) in beautiful surroundings.

Another obvious object of idolatry is the car. Like alcohol, it is an especially worrying idolatry in that it exacts a daily toll of human sacrifice, young and old, costlier and bloodier than that demanded by the Minotaur (a prototype that was wisely confined in a labyrinth). The human wreckage left by worship of the bottle and the car raises grave questions about the degree of our supposed civilization. The cost of our idolatries is pinpointed in the contrast between the idyllicism of the advertisements for bottle and car and the scenes in the wards where DT cases and human vegetables are confined. Few would question that use of the car has got out of rational human control. When it becomes manifestly quicker to walk than to drive somewhere (as in our inner cities), then plainly something has gone wrong. When every expansion of our road system is followed by parallel (or greater) expansion in the size and number of vehicles in transit, then even the least skeptical thinker smells a rat.

Nor is this the greatest paradox. There are urban areas where it is not safe to walk because pedestrians are easy prey for assailants and muggers. You would be in danger of menace or assault if you walked, so, for safety's sake, you drive. In other words, you get into your car (your metal box) for the very same reason that the medieval knight got into his armor (his metal box) and climbed on to horseback at the start of a journey. Like him, you are safer encased in sheet metal, travelling at a speed faster than human legs can achieve, with a horsepower at your disposal that can scatter or trample upon potential assailants. Here we touch the irony by which a new invention can turn back the clock of history and reverse the evolutionary process. Man, the rational biped, adopts the form of the four-wheeled monster that roars and rushes about the streets with its toughly protective hide of steel plate. This effects a reversal of evolution. For often enough, as the physical power of man is increased by the motor vehicle, so his brainpower (in terms of judgment and reason) is correspondingly diminished, his moral sense of responsibility is atrophied, and his human sensibilities in relation to the sufferings and failings of others are numbed. The brain of the monster is minute, for it varies in inverse proportion to its strength. Even so, man-in-car and man-in-truck may become virtually composite creatures of dinosaurian character and dimensions, the brain being reduced to microscopic proportions relative to the tough hide and monstrous motive power.

Idolatries take basically healthy human interests and activities, and debase them by perversion and excess. This applies notably to the now vast and multifarious idolatry represented by pop music. No one can deny that the hagiology, the festive celebrations, the dissemination of icons, the cherishing of tokens, the rituals of commemoration, and the prostration of personality in adoration involved in the cult of pop stars are features borrowed from the religious sphere. The extremes of behavior involved in the cult of the least respectable pop stars may well remind us of the obscene rites associated with those pagan divinities from whom the Old Testament prophets called upon the people to turn their hearts.

This idolatry is an especially detestable stain upon our civilization because it involves the corruption of the young on a massive scale. Indeed the moral and educational problem represented by the cult of pop music seems to me perhaps the most underestimated social menace of the day. The young have a limited amount of time and energy available for development of potential talent and understanding to fit them for self-enrichment and the enrichment of others in a world offering immense opportunities for worthwhile achievement. Thus the problem of the sheer number of valuable teenage hours consumed in the inert assimilation of inanities and the quantity of valuable teenage energy wasted in the hysteria of misdirected adulation surely becomes, at a certain stage, something other than an amusing matter at which the educated among us can shrug our shoulders in detachment.

Let us ask ourselves the question: By whose will does it obtain —

by whose conscious wish and intention does it obtain — that depraved young men and women, often wholly talentless and shameless, near maniacs in some cases, should be paid for their self-indulgence and their corruption of the young the kind of incomes that could irrigate vast deserts and keep hungry cities fed if the money were appropriately applied? By whose will and intention? We know the answer of course. By the will and intention of faceless entrepreneurs who, for financial gain, exploit the human body and the human emotions as recklessly as do those who profiteer by prostitution. Do we want this exploitation of our young? And, if we don't, why can't we get rid of it? Where is the sense in financing expensive educational systems professedly devoted to the enrichment of our cultural life with one hand, and with the other engineering the degradation of the young by pouring into their homes a perpetual flood of aural drivel? Here again, in this reversion to irrational devaluation of human potential, we seem to see the spectacle of civilizational regress.

The current condition of our civilization and its idolatries brings into question the notion of a one-way movement of history on which most of us were brought up. We have touched already on the popular illusion that the newest thing is the best thing. This, of course, is only one aspect of the wider assumption that modern civilization is a one-way process of continuing improvement. The historian and the philosopher are aware, not only that behind us lie both periods of ascent and periods of decline, but also that a gain in one area of development may be matched by a loss in another. For example, hardly anyone would question that great strides have been made in medical science during the last hundred years. But who can say whether the vast ameliorative effects of these developments have been counterbalanced by the widespread abuse of drugs that medical science has made available? The price civilization may yet have to pay for the contraceptive pill is unknown. One would not wish to be a scaremonger over issues like this, but Nature has a habit of wreaking vengeance for any tampering with her delicately balanced mechanisms, as the deserts of North Africa and North America testify. It took a long time for the damage done by tobacco to come to light. We are only just beginning to be able to reckon the physical and mental cost of the gasoline engine. We have learned that pesticides and insecticides are double-edged weapons. Evidence such as this suggests that what science and technology achieve in one direction may be counterbalanced by the damage they do in other directions so that, although the achievements are real and beneficial, the general lot of man, in so far as it is measurable, is not improving at the rate these achievements suggest.

The media today devote their energies to proclaiming the message that civilization is always getting better. This is their proclamation; indeed it is their peculiar gospel. The Christian philosopher is likely to see in this notion a kind of super-idolatry, an "umbrella-idolatry" sheltering many lesser idolatries. Indeed the idolatry of Progress is a more menacing idolatry than any we have yet touched upon. Things like cars and drink, fashion and pop music, gambling and pornography, even career-making and money-making, can be readily recognized as idolatries, but worship of Progress, which is an intellectual matter not superficially evidenced in the satisfaction of appetite or the possession of goods, is an altogether subtler and more insidious idolatry in that it softens up the mind to the thoughtless acceptance of error and illusion.

This idolatry has infiltrated the Christian community to an alarming degree. Its undercover operations are sinister and far-reaching. While it may be hard to raise in a believer's mind the suspicion that a Christian doctrine or practice is false or meaningless, it is not difficult to prove that it is "old" or that it "derives from the past," for in fact most good things do, from wine and symphonies to paintings and valuable furniture. And if the mind has been softened up to ready acquiescence in the notion that what is "old" or "derivative from the past" will generally (despite the evidence of the auction room or the library) be inferior to what is "new" and "pointing to the future," then the weaning of heart from attachment to things reliable and worthy is already half-accomplished. For instance, it is clearly because of this insidious grip of the idolatry of progress that it has proved possible of late to foist upon congregations of faithful Christians versions of the Bible and liturgical forms in literary terms sadly inferior to those they supersede.

The public has been fed for decades on the modern myth of

Cumulative Emancipation. This myth, an aspect of the idolatry of Inevitable Progress, presents every step forward in the intellectual, the social, or the political field as a movement in the universal process of emancipation. Workers are emancipated from slavery to capitalists, women from servitude to men, children from work in factories, students from academic disciplines, citizens from the threat of poverty, believers from the chains of dogma, artists from the fetters of censorship, women from the tyranny of ovulation, homosexuals from laws against perversion, couples from the prison of lifelong marriage, pregnant women from consequent labor.

Whatever restriction we get rid of, its removal is accounted a good thing. That is "progress." The past which stretches out behind us is vaguely conceived as centuries of increasing blackness during which the human race was so trapped, fettered, chained, strait-jacketed, and bullied that it seems remarkable that anyone had the freedom and initiative to build, write, paint, and compose the artistic masterpieces that somehow, in spite of all the strangulation of individuality, managed to get created. Of course the past presupposed by the idolators of progress never existed. We may hope that the myth of Cumulative Emancipation likewise presupposes a future that will never exist. The alternative is too dreadful to contemplate: a future of escalating derestrictions stretching before us, vistas of expanding "freedoms" in which eventually sodomy in public will be as acceptable a pastime as cricket and female nudity will be so widespread that women in copes and miters will look old-fashioned.

There is no one-way progress. The present is a "phase." It is a phase which may be succeeded by an intensification of its tendencies or by a harsh reaction against its tendencies. The one thing that seems to be absolutely certain, judging from the experience of the past, is that the next age is going to ridicule and despise us. And those of us who are most completely "of our age" will be most scornfully despised. Whether the next age will ridicule us for being fuddy-duddies who lacked the courage to go the whole hog in blasting away inhibitions on the march of increasing per-missiveness, or whether the next age will scorn us for our decadent betrayal of civilized standards of decency and restraint, is a question we cannot answer. But one can say this: If there is a reaction against our morals, sexual behavior, and sexual display, it will not be the first time, for there has certainly been no one-way movement in this respect during the past few centuries.

In the late 1940s I had a student who got interested in the history of the English novel and read the novels of Aphra Behn, the Restoration writer. He decided to sample her plays and asked for them at a certain well-known library of some standing in the literary world. The plays were regarded as licentious, and the librarian was at first reluctant to put them into the young man's hands, even when assured that he was a *bona fide* student of English Literature. This odd anecdote is recounted, not to highlight the difference between the 1940s and the 1980s, but to highlight the difference between the 1940s and the 1670s and 1680s when the plays were first performed. Within the lifetimes of some of us there was a period when the popular mind had to look at the past, not just as containing tyrannies from which progress had emancipated us, but also as containing freedoms which progress had gradually denied us. The myth of one-way cumulative emancipation will not do.

There is on my shelves an edition of the plays of Sir John Vanbrugh, another Restoration dramatist, which was published in 1896 with some notes by a Victorian editor. Of the play, *The Relapse*, he writes that it contains some very noble sentiments and some characters which "redeem to a great extent whatever may be condemned as immoral in the piece, *from our modern point of view*" (my italics). Thus, in 1896, the modern point of view finds the drama of the 1690s immoral, but is prepared to overlook this defect in view of the "noble sentiments" and virtuous characters which are also represented. It appears that the "modern point of view" is after all not always a progressively more liberal, emancipated, and uncensorious one than the older point of view. Indeed, one may question whether the standards of the 1690s or those of the 1890s in this respect resembled more what might be called the "moral norm." The Restoration period was a period of great moral looseness and permissiveness in London society. We are told of Charles II receiving people in audience while toying with his mistress's nipples. Moralists of the age had much the same kind of thing to say about contemporary decadence and permissiveness as our own moralists today. Dryden made a fierce attack in 1686 upon the prostitution of literature effected in the obscenities of contemporary drama:

> O wretched we! why were we hurried down
> This lubrique and adulterate age,
> (Nay added fat pollution of our own)
> To increase the steaming ordures of the stage?

Yet Vanbrugh's play, *The Relapse*, would not raise many eyebrows today. Does that make us the beneficiaries of an emancipated culture or of an insensitively coarsened one?

The question is asked because of the peculiar history of this particular play. Richard Sheridan was no prude, but when he wanted to revive Vanbrugh's *The Relapse* some seventy years later in 1777, he had to rewrite it as *A Trip to Scarborough* because the public of the day, and that meant London society of course, would not tolerate Vanbrugh's coarseness. "Some plays may justly call for alteration," says Sheridan's prologue, speaking of the need to "draw some slender covering" over what was "too bare before":

> Those writers well and wisely use their pens
> Who turn our wantons into Magdalens.

Will it happen again? That is the interesting question. Will our second age of licentiousness in the post-Reformation era pass away like the first one? Will our grandchildren and great grandchildren look back on the 1960s, 1970s and 1980s as later eighteenth and nineteenth century society looked back on the Restoration period? If we ourselves do not shudder at the licentiousness of Restoration dissolutes because indeed we are in the same boat, is this something for which the future will downgrade us?

Our ignorance of what the future will say of us has interesting implications. We really do not know, for instance, whether ardent campaigners like England's Mary Whitehouse, who demand the cleaning up of entertainment and the rehabilitation of sexual morality, are reactionaries or progressives. If the decades at the turn of the century are to be more permissive than our own, then such campaigners are reactionaries, resisting the trend of the times. But if the decades at the turn of the century are to be less permissive and more disciplined than our own, then they are forward-looking progressives who have forecast the shape of the future, seeing ahead of their generation.

The effect of successful education is to widen horizons. First the schoolchild discovers that his parents' views are not the only views, then that the attitudes and manners of his social class are not the only attitudes and manners, that the habits of thought of his home locality are not the only habits of thought. The maturing student has to learn, step by step, to submit criteria and presuppositions that he has been brought up with to the judgment of other classes, creeds, localities, nationalities. A most crucial step, when he has learned to see his own class as only one among classes, his own nationality as only one among nationalities, his own creed as only one among creeds, is the step which reveals to him that his own age is only one among ages, that his age is a phase, that what it automatically thinks, assumes, and teaches may be wrong. This realization is what marks off the really educated man from the half-educated. The educated man has a sense of the present, not as a finality, not as the climax of history, not as the true basis for judgment on all other ages, not even in any respect as a "reliable norm," but as a passing phase that is no more likely than any other past phase to be free of prejudices and biases that distort sound judgment.

No one in our century has been more persuasive than T.S. Eliot in warning of the fallacy of trying to disown the past and in dismantling popular notions of inevitable progress. "Encouraged by superficial notions of evolution," Eliot observes, we tend to think of life as a process of continuous development. We mentally cast off the past and grasp at the future. Encouraged by the media to assume that every age is better than its predecessor, there are those who always apply words like "old," "traditional" and "established" to things they disapprove of, while they use words like "new" and "forward-looking," not just as descriptive terms but as expressions of approval. Our public values in the political field tend to hinge upon an idealized future. We are always just about to get through a crisis. We are always temporarily putting up with difficulties in order to overcome them completely next year or the year after. We are always going through a hard time in order to reach a good time. The older people among us, having listened to this kind of talk through so many decades and learned by bitter experience that the good time when the crisis is behind us never actually arrives, tend to get sour and cynical about the whole dream of progress to a better world. They look back to the days of their youth, when they were hopeful and idealistic, and they tend to conclude that civilization is going downhill.

So, on the one hand we have those, the majority, who believe in inevitable progress and shake off the past. They see the future in a rosy glow. It contains the summation of all improvements patiently registered by society from year to year. On the other hand we have those who, in reaction against this view, appear to believe in inevitable regress, and assume that every age is worse than its predecessor. They write letters to the press complaining about modern youth or the Welfare State and reminding us of what things were like when they were young. They agitate against expressways, fluoride, and the erection of public housing in picturesque villages. They are nostalgic for steam trains, deserted roads, organ-grinders, frequent postal deliveries, guineas and half-crowns. Where the idolators of progress idealize the future, the idolators of regress idealize the past. The danger is that if you disagree with someone who is fixated on the future (as we have just been doing most violently), he will assume that you are fixated on the past; and if you disagree with someone who is fixated on the past, he will assume that you are fixated on the future. The truth of the matter is that idealizers of the future and idealizers of the past have much in common and are really very close together. They both misconceive the past; one seeing it as blacker than it was; the other seeing it as whiter than it was. They share a common insensitivity to the past as it really was, and a common misunderstanding of the way the present is involved with it. Those who believe that things are always getting better and those who believe that things are always getting worse are really in the same boat. Both kinds of people evade the present, the one to focus on a dream future, the other to focus on a dream past.

A book such as this, which attempts to analyze the present with

Christian penetration and which, in so doing, finds it necessary to puncture prevalent popular assumptions about inevitable progress, will readily be misunderstood — and could be readily misinterpreted — as one more cry of lamentation on a declining Church and a declining age from a writer enamored of the past. It is therefore absolutely essential to reiterate the point that the writer sees the worshippers of the past and the worshippers of the future as idolators guilty of a common idolatry. If one lays stress on the evils of the present, one must not be assumed to believe that the past was necessarily any better. The man who can see through his own age and not see through past ages is as much a dreamer as the man who worships his own age or who believes that there will be pie in the sky in the future. The realist — and the thoughtful Christian is the surest realist of all — takes account of the defects and inadequacies of the human situation over against eternity. His standard is the kingdom of God; judged by that standard, there is no certainty that any age of history is going to show up as utterly finer, or as more decadent, than our own.

What applies to overall judgments on past ages applies to judgments on the Church in particular. If we have escaped from the naive notion that the Church on earth is getting better every day, every year, every century, only to embrace the equally naive notion that the Church on earth is getting worse every day, every year, every century, then we have jumped from the frying pan of idolatrous future-worship into the fire of idolatrous past-worship. Here in England the journalists like to write columns testifying to the "decline" of the Church of England. Decline from what? That is the question to ask oneself on coming across one of these columns. Which was the age of accepted Anglican — or even Christian — vitality and energy from whose peak the Church is now slithering into the depths? I have just read in T.F. Powys' story, *Hester Dominy*, "The old women went to church as usual and the men stayed away." That was village life in Somerset recorded in the 1920s with a backward glance, and it was obviously not very different from what we know today. Do we have to look a bit further back to find the heights from which the Church has slithered into the depths? Is the peak period of Anglican well-being supposed to have been the Victorian Age? Anyone who has read the novels of Trollope would have reservations about the idea. Anyone who has read, say, E.F. Benson's autobiographical book, *As We Were*, subtitled *A Victorian Peep-Show*, would scoff at the idea. Benson, of course, was the son of E.W. Benson, Headmaster of Wellington College, then Bishop of Truro, and eventually Archbishop of Canterbury. Read E.F.'s account of the state of his diocese when his father went to Truro in 1877. Learn how parish priests were treating their responsibilities, how entrenched some of them were in lazy neglect of duty. Then ask yourself where are the parish priests today who sit tight in their livings and scarcely ever go near the church whose incumbency they hold.

It is questionable whether anyone can point to a period when the worship and practice of the Church of England were generally such that they could be held up as models from which today's worship and practice represent a grave decline. No doubt more people attended church services in Victorian days. We know what church attendance meant in terms of moral pressure upon peasants and workers, and in terms of social convention among the middle classes. We used to hear a good deal about the menace of "nominal Christianity." It seems that with declining church attendance we have now got rid of one feature of "nominal Christianity" and, as a consequence, we begin to talk about the Church's decline. Perhaps, in this respect too, small is beautiful.

Numerical fall-off in worship, however, is by no means the only matter at issue. People point to the antics of way-out clerics and claim that the Church is going to the dogs. Without wishing to condone offences against decent order in worship and against sheer common sense in parochial practice, one may question whether our parsons are less stable than their predecessors in a calling which has always had its share of eccentrics. Individualists, positive and negative in their idiosyncrasies, have always adorned English incumbencies. We may be taken aback to find a modern parson's proclivities being lampooned in a dramatic study like that of the Reverend Ossian Flint in David Mercer's play, *Flint*. Seventy-year-old Ossian is a shocker, and his questionable relationship with a delinquent girl takes a bit of swallowing. "His appetites are grotesque," his own bishop concedes. But Flint is a wit, and he is not a hypocrite, and that is more than could be said, say, of Jane Austen's Mr. Collins in *Pride and Prejudice*. One may question whether a clerical scene that provokes a satirist to the creation of an Ossian Flint is more corrupt than a clerical scene that provokes a satirist to the creation of a Mr. Collins. What of the snobberies of the Edwardian cathedral close pilloried in Hugh Walpole's *The Cathedral* (on the basis of first-hand experience at Durham)? What of the village parson in T.F. Powys' *Kindness in a Corner* who has to rush around on the morning of a bishop's visit to rustle up a confirmation candidate and who finds an obliging parishioner long accustomed to submit to the ceremony at regular intervals as the honor of the parish seems to require?

Perhaps it is dangerous to try to argue a case on the basis of how clergy are represented in fiction and drama. Often enough the prissy clerical stereotype of comedy, like Canon Chasuble in Wilde's *The Importance of Being Earnest*, is a mere comic device, no more representative of the Church than the stage village constable is of the Police Force. Nevertheless acceptable images have to have some recognizable connection with reality, even if it is a twisted or inverted one, and the clergy are certainly not faring in literature worse than they were. Not that they ever fared very well. Certainly there is nothing in literature to suggest that fifty or a hundred years ago the parson was a generally revered and devout individual superior to the passions and the little-mindedness that mar the lives of his fellows. The literature of the time often put him under fierce attack. Somerset Maugham had a vicarage upbringing and, in his autobiographical novel, *Of Human Bondage*, published in 1915, he got revenge by picturing his hero's Uncle Willie as a narrow-minded, repressive clergyman, and just the fellow to destroy a young boy's faith. Twenty years later George Orwell, in *A Clergyman's Daughter*, not only turned the heroine's father into a caricature of selfishness and insensitivity, but also included among the social outcasts who haunt Trafalgar Square during the night hours an unfrocked clergyman, Mr. Tallboys, eloquent and ingenious in his blasphemies.

One suspects, attending to the printed word, that we have no cause at all to claim that our clergy of the 1980s are on the whole less worthy, devout, wise, or, indeed, educated than their predecessors. The prevalent weaknesses of the clergy, and of all men, no doubt change from age to age. Our clergy today are surely less worldly than many of their predecessors in pursuit of money and status, or they would never have got ordained. There is nothing in today's ecclesiastical setup to lure lovers of comfort and social position into the priesthood. And certainly our clergy have no opportunity to be as repressive as some of their predecessors appear to have been. Allowing for the exaggerations of anti-clerical writers like Maugham and Orwell, we need only recall Charlotte Bronte's Mr. Brocklehurst in *Jane Eyre* to remind ourselves that the repressive clergyman of fiction was not always a fantastic invention conjured up out of malice. If we have problem parsons today, it is not that they ape Mr. Brocklehurst. In this respect they are in line with the rest of us. We do not make quite the same mistakes as our predecessors. Indeed we shun them with such determination and self-consciousness that we fail to notice ourselves making mistakes of a converse kind. We are determined not to be as repressive as our grandfathers and great grandfathers, and we are so zealous in not being repressive that we tend to be over-indulgent. We are so anxious not to appear puritanical that we fail to discourage licentiousness. And when our own children and grandchildren turn on us, it will be with satirical judgments very different from those we pass on our fathers and grandfathers; very different in character, that is, yet in spirit and in essence repeating a familiar rhythm of response and counter-response that has recurred through the ages.

Journalistic accounts of the supposed "decline" of the Church mostly turn on quite other matters than this of the quality of the clergy. They often convey a vague impression of a looseness of authority and discipline, a flabbiness of conviction, and a feeling of ineffectiveness in the struggle against unbelief. Now all these are weaknesses of the Church which this book has focused upon. But this book has not, therefore, spoken of the decline of the Church. For to speak of the decline of the Church in this connection would be to imply a past phase of comparative well-being for the Church on earth from which the declension set in. While we must not soft-pedal any of the shortcomings of the Church in the present, we must not pretend that there were not comparable shortcomings in the past. Perhaps the point could be made most forcibly by a concrete instance. Over 250 years ago Jonathan Swift wrote a dazzling little tract in which he argued against the abolition of Christianity, and it provides material that will illuminate our case. Its full title is: "An Argument to prove that the Abolishing of Christianity in England may, as things stand, be attended with some inconveniences, and perhaps not produce those many good effects proposed thereby."

Swift, of course, was an Irishman, but he was in England when this tract was written. Though he moved back to Dublin in 1701 and became Dean of St. Patrick's Cathedral there in 1713, there were long stretches in between when he was in London engaged in political business for men at the top. The pamphlet in question was written about 1709 or 1710 at a time when he was intimately conversant with the English social and political scene at its center. It is an exercise in irony, of which Swift was the supreme master. In his most notorious exercise in the ironic vein, the famous pamphlet, "A Modest Proposal," he urged a novel and permanent solution of the Irish question upon the English. It was that the poverty-stricken lot of the Irish peasantry could be alleviated if their babies were fattened for consumption at the table. The babies were commended for their nutritive value, and culinary details were supplied. An advantageous by-product of introducing the babies into the diet would be that the proportion of papists in Ireland would be thereby reduced.

There is no comparable savagery of indignation in the essay against abolishing Christianity, but there is the same poker-faced irony; for Swift's method is to reply, point by point, to imaginary opponents who are supposed to have made a cogent case for abolishing Christianity. Let us examine what he has to say.

Firstly, he concedes the weakness of his case in trying to defend the preservation of Christianity at a time when all powerful influences seem determined to abolish it. Yet he has talked with older people, he remarks with some surprise, who assure him that it would at one time have appeared just as eccentric to want to destroy Christianity as it now appears to want to preserve it. Of course, Swift goes on, it must be understood that he is not being so foolish as to argue in favor of *real* Christianity, the thing that existed in primitive times and indeed (if contemporary records can be trusted) actually "had an influence upon men's beliefs and actions." No, no. To attempt to revive that would be to blow current civilization to pieces. So all he is seeking to preserve is "nominal Christianity," the real thing "having been for some time wholly laid aside by general consent, as utterly inconsistent with our present schemes of wealth and power."

Among the supposed points that have to be answered, Swift tackles the argument that abolishing Christianity would make one day more per week available for "trade, business and pleasure" and enable many useful buildings to be converted into theaters, commercial exchanges, and assembly halls. Swift replies to this case by pointing out that these are exactly the kind of purposes for which churches are used anyway as it is; they already fulfill the functions of theaters, exchanges, and assembly halls; everybody uses them for making social contacts and for flirting, for showing off fine clothes, fixing up business deals, and catching up on sleep. Handing the churches over therefore would make no practical difference in this respect.

Swift then tackles his imaginary opponent's argument that it is a ridiculous way of running a country to employ a set of men to bawl one day of the week against the methods that absolutely everybody employs on the other six days for getting on in life and having a good time. The argument falls down, he says. For this propaganda of the parsons, by presenting what everyone does as being forbidden, adds to the excitement of doing it and prevents life from being tedious and boring.

He then turns to the argument that getting rid of Christianity will remove from the educational system all indoctrination of virtues and values which inhibit people from yielding to their instincts and appetites. This, says Swift, is an utterly outmoded argument. For the evidence is that contemporary education has already ceased to inculcate any respect at all for virtues and values of any kind, and the products of the system obviously are already totally devoid of any principles that might inhibit them from doing exactly what they feel like doing. Abolishing Christianity would thus not make any difference at all.

Turning to the question of the common people, Swift dissociates himself from those who think religion is the dope of the masses, invented by politicians to keep the lower classes docile. For the evidence is to the contrary. The English working class, he proclaims, are as staunch a body of unbelievers as the upper class themselves. He notes, however, that Christianity *does* contain a few notions that are useful for keeping children quiet and passing the time on tedious winter evenings. Abolishing Christianity would be inconvenient to parents in this respect. Moreover it would be disadvantageous to the general public in that, by removing parsons from the human scene, it would deprive people of a stock object of entertainment by mockery and ridicule. Finally, to crown his case, Swift tackles with devastating irony the question: Would abolishing Christianity seriously damage the Church? And he has to concede that, indeed, it might prove a first step towards transforming the Church for the worse.

There are, of course, paragraphs in Swift's essay which strike the reader like a voice from a far-off age. But the points selected here are central to the argument, and they might have been made yesterday. They are: Swift's disgust at the thinness of nominal Christianity; his emphasis on the gaping abyss between deeply effective Christian commitment and the contemporary social, commercial, and political scene; his protest against meaningless church attendance; his critique of current educational practice and the kind of mentality it produces; his mockery of the idea that the mass of the population are believers; and his ridicule of the notion that there is a necessary connection between Christianity and the Church.

Two points emerge from this account of Swift's essay. The first is that the Church of England was probably in no better condition in 1710 than it is in the 1980s; that it was possibly in a much worse condition in 1710 than it is in the 1980s; that Christianity probably had no deeper roots among the English public in 1710 than it has in the 1980s; that in short, whatever else may be said, the Church of England can scarcely be claimed to have declined over the centuries between. The second point to emerge from consideration of Swift's essay is that radicals and the rest of those who make a big noise are utterly wrong when they imply that the Church has lacked acute self-criticism, criticism from within, until they came along to provide it. The Church has always been self-critical.

Swift's pamphlet provides an excellent example of what often confronts the reader when he turns aside from talk of progress or talk of decline and actually examines the work of wise Christians of the past. He meets with something which compels him to say, not "How much better things were then," nor "How much worse things were then," but "How similar things were deep down." For the Christian's grave problems vis-à-vis the world have a basically similar character from century to century. What changes is not the essential nature of the spiritual or moral conflict, but the external mode in which it is expressed. It ought not to surprise us that this is the case, that we should find Christian writers of the past saying the same things essentially about their own day as we say about our day. If this were not the case, the study of great thinkers like Augustine and Aquinas, or great writers like Dante and Milton, would be of limited academic and historical interest; whereas indeed these writers speak to us in our situation all the more power-fully because their problems are basically ours though their exter-nal fashions are so fascinatingly different.

This is not to deny that there have been ages in which Christians have had to face pains and difficulties which we, at least in the West today, are happily spared. But even in centuries of overt or official persecution, the problems of Christians were not so much different in kind from ours as different in degree and intensity; different in respect of the physical or mental consequences of making a stand. It remains in essentials the same issue which faces the Christian who is challenged to stand by his beliefs whether the penalty for standing firm is to be thrown to the lions in Nero's Rome, to be exiled to Siberia in Stalin's Russia, or to be denied a medical career in gynecology in contemporary England because of refusal to commit or condone the murder of the unborn.

Christians have always accepted that their spiritual and moral position vis-à-vis the unbelieving world does not in essentials change. Our reliance upon the Bible as the word of God presup-poses that advice given in one age is valid for another. The pattern of Christian preaching established over the centuries is based on the assumption that the Christian message is unalterable in its essentials. You take a text from the Bible, a passage of exhortation, or a parable, and you proceed to expound its implications for men and women working in the world of the 1980s. (How interesting it is that the sermon which starts from the Old or New Testament generally proves so much more deeply relevant than the one that starts from something in yesterday's newspaper.) The doctrine of the Incarnation loses its power and its comprehensiveness if it is assumed that what is said in one age must lose its relevance in another. It is no accident, therefore, that the doctrine of the Incarnation should tend to come under question among relativists who worship change and devalue spiritual stability. If truth and value changed with the changing centuries, then a succession of Christs would be needed to make clear God's ways with men.

6

Where do we stand against irrationalism?

OURS IS NOT an age in which the rationalist attack upon Christianity is a predominant problem. By and large, thinkers are not trying to argue Christians into atheism by logical reasoning to which Christians can reply in kind. The old arguments proving the existence of God by reasoning from the evidence of Nature, human understanding, and human history are not being called for. Rather they are being discredited in advance by positivistic thinking or bypassed by existential relativism—the various philosophical attitudes which assume that human life is something that we make up as we go along. As a consequence, because rational analysis is not being applied to the overall problems of the nature of being and the purpose of human life, least of all by enemies of Christianity, the danger is that we Christians will fall into the prevailing habit and ignore the rational basis of our faith; that we shall allow the tools of logic and reason to rust; and ourselves cultivate the fashion of justifying belief in terms of instant experience and inadequately defined subjectivist well-being.

One hears, both at the popular level and at the middlebrow level, both via the media and within educational circles, a kind of pseudo-thinking which is deeply imbrued with subjectivism so capricious and relativisms so fluid as to defy analysis and to render potential argument null. Only last night I heard a characteristic specimen of this pseudo-thinking in a radio interview with a fashion designer; one might hear similar instances any night of the week in comparable interviews or discussions about the arts or about social affairs. Asked to account for past successes in the launching of new styles, the fashion designer had recourse to expressions like "It was alive" and "It was relevant" and "It anticipated a trend." These expressions were voiced as approval-noises without any awareness that, for the logical mind, they require some objective point of repose. Hitler was once very much *alive.* The attack on Pearl Harbor was highly *relevant* to the careers of many Americans. The initial Nazi propaganda against the Jews correctly *anticipated the trend* that brought the gas chambers and mass graves of Dachau. On what basis of sense and logic do we now choose to use the terms "alive," "relevant" and "correctly anticipative of a trend" as approval noises rather than disapproval noises?

The habit of making judgments in such terms as "It was good because...." "It was true in that....," or "It was beautiful in respect of...," now derided in some circles, compelled human beings to evaluate on rational grounds by reference to standards with objective validity. What do we gain by cultivating a vocabulary of approval ("He/It was alive," "He/It was relevant," "He/It correctly anticipated the trend") which could with equal accuracy be applied to heroic saints or criminal tyrants, to acts of creativity or deeds of unspeakable horror and destruction? Yet we find criticism of the arts, for instance, riddled with the kind of approval noises exemplified above which leave the rational mind aghast at the prevailing illiteracy of the media world. I heard some in discussions last week on new plays and novels. "Did it tick?" "Oh yes, it ticked." (A grandfather clock ticks. So does a time-bomb.) "Did it say something?" "Oh yes, it said something." (Shakespeare says something. Goebbels said an awful lot.) "Is it a breakthrough?" "Oh yes, it's a breakthrough." (Space technology has made a break-through. Rabies has made a breakthrough.) "Did it disturb you?" "Oh yes, it disturbed me." (Conscience disturbs one. Cancer also disturbs one.) "Does it shock?" "Oh yes, it shocks." (The divine voice can shock. So can maniacal obscenity.)

These approval-noises can be heard any night of the week or read any day of the week by courtesy of the media, and they represent a total intellectual bankruptcy. Approval noises which could be equally applicable to the finest specimens of good or the worst examples of evil are evasive of rational thought. They are a part of the machinery of decomposition by which the values of Western Christendom are being eroded from within. There is a vocabulary of approval and disapproval now in use at the admittedly semi-literate level of current journalism and broadcast-ing which exudes the emotive flavor appropriate to asserting or negating value, and yet this vocabulary is in fact devoid of any genuine evaluative content at all. Let us return to that interview about fashions. The strongest approval-noises accompanied such statements as "I want dresses that enable the wearer to say 'This is me.' " (Where is the dress that would prevent the wearer from saying "This is me?"); "Clothes should say, 'Look at me: I'm a woman.' " (Where are the clothes that would say, "Look the other way: I'm a cow?"); "Women want to go about being themselves." (What would turn them into something else?); "Women want to be what they are." (Can they help it?). The reader will be able to supplement this list of examples with parallels from his own experience. An idiom has become fashionable which consists entirely of tautologies. (A woman is a woman is a woman.) There is no intention here to apply heavy-handed criticism to habits of speech which are flippantly or wryly used at a consciously superficial level in relation to such lighthearted matters as those of fashion. The trouble is that this thoughtless usage is symptomatic of deeper ills. For both of the verbal devices we have just illustrated (the evasion of objectivity and the exploitation of virtual tautology) have in fact established themselves as modes of utterance applicable to graver and more momentous issues. We meet them even in the religious sphere. The kind of frivolous subjectivities and tautologies appropriate to lighthearted chatter about new films or new fashions are transmuted into ostensibly sober criticisms of serious matters. For instance, a form of worship in a traditional liturgy is said to be faulty "because it does not speak to me" and a petition or a confession judged inadequate because "somehow it isn't me." The proper reply to such observations is clearly that an act of worship is not meant to speak to the worshipper, but to God, who is probably less inhibited than we are about what he can or cannot take in — after centuries of listening to human worship. Similarly a petition or a confession — or any other act of prayer — is intended to lift us out of ourselves, and the more "it isn't me," the better, roughly speaking.

The reader may protest that a sledgehammer is being used to crack a nut, but the implications involved in the acceptance of the subjective and the tautological as appropriate modes of Christian utterance are vast. I have a Church journal before me in which a writer proclaims "to be a Christian is to be human," which of course says nothing at all, since "to be a murderer is to be human," the crime being impossible for an animal. But the tautology having been accepted, it is easy, by a series of false deductions to move from "to be a Christian is to be human," to "this or that sin is only human" and to "to be a Christian is to commit this or that sin without shame." The actual increase in this kind of irrationalism is worrying chiefly because the machinery of reason is being increasingly neglected in the pulpit, the religious press, and even in religious educational circles.

The Christian bulwark against nonsense of this kind is the doctrine of Creation. The doctrine of Creation is not only about the fact that God made the world, for it assumes that God made the world with a purpose. An interesting feature of the Creation myth as recorded in the book of Genesis is the orderliness of the record. The story is a story of logical design carried through in due sequence. The creation is phased. For the doctrine of Creation is not exhausted when you have derived from it the notion of a divine First Cause. There is also the notion of design and purpose. God fashioned the world with a design and purpose built into the whole scheme from the start.

It is important to stress this fact in our day and age. Christianity commits us to the concept of an ordered, meaningful, purposeful world. By virtue of the doctrine of Creation, Christianity has a vested interest in those notions of order and objectivity, meaning and purpose, which are currently at a discount in the kind of fashionable thinking I have exemplified. The approval-noises and disapproval-noises of current relativism and subjectivism are antithetical to the Christian notion of an ordered universe created by God to serve his good purposes. They are congruous with the notion of a cosmic flux within which our human careers are so many limpid fluidities, attaining casual significance only in so far as the topography of riverbed and bank, or the contact of fish and weed, brings about in us a ripple, a froth or a bubble, here one moment, and gone the next.

A Christian understands human life very differently. It is a pilgrimage through time to eternity, a pilgrimage whose every adventure encountered, every contact made, every inch of terrain traversed, offers one more possiblity for playing a part in God's grand design, and indeed can be meaningfully interpreted only in relation to the touch of a purpose extending beyond the confines of our individual lives and beyond the limit of our racial lives. This is, of course, a remarkable statement to make. It implies that anything and everything you do today can be truly interpreted and justly valued only against standards and criteria operative beyond the limits of the temporal universe. That sounds rather abstruse and metaphysical, but it only puts into philosophical terminology truths which are much more lucidly and happily phrased in the simple Christian teaching about doing God's will and serving his purposes. We accept these simple teachings in the sense that we take them in with our ears and nod assent to them in the brain. But are we sufficiently awake to the fact that, accepting such teachings, we have *ipso facto* excluded a gigantic mass of fashionable notions that cumber the minds of our contemporaries? Obviously if the meaning of our earthly course, and all the little daily thoughts and acts that make it up, is discernable only by reference to the will and purpose of a God who created us and everything of which we are a part, then the attempt to interpret the experience of any passing moment in terms of the kind of approval-noises and disapproval-noises I have referred to is simply absurd. It will not do to judge anything at all by recourse to relativist and subjectivist whims and feelings. Put crudely, it will not do to be forever thinking in terms of "Is this really me?" or "Does this grab me?" or "Do I dig it?" or whatever is the latest jargon in the life-is-froth-and-I'm-just-a-bubble game.

While one must not simply take issue with casual conversational habits we use lightheartedly for approving of a glass of beer or a new blouse, one must stress that, at a deep level, even the glass of beer and the new blouse can be *justly* valued as products of God's creative work for which we rightly give thanks, which we properly enjoy and appreciate. And because the glass of beer and the new blouse are different in degree of bounty and blessedness from, say, the happy marriage or the gift of a child, we must not therefore think that for the greater blessing one is accountable to God and for the lesser blessing not so. Indeed if we solemnly give thanks at the wedding service or the baptismal service for the major divine bounties, and then treat the minor bounties as though they were not matters within the divine purview but rather matters whose significance can be fully reckoned with in terms of whether they tickle our feelings enough, we reveal our spiritual obtuseness.

This is not an argument in support of ponderous solemnity in connection with the lighter and minor pleasures of life. Rather it is a warning that if we establish a habit of response to the comparatively trivial delights of life in terms of the titillation of appetite or ego, the habit can grow and become our norm of response in bigger and more momentous matters. One can see this process in operation in the world of the media. The voice that approves the new fashion "because it does something to me" can very soon be approving a Beethoven symphony "because it does something to me." Soon after that the voice can be approving a magnificent cathedral, a beautiful ceremony, a great book, a heroic deed, a mighty communal venture on the same grounds. This should make the absurdity, the vanity, the enormity of the subjective evaluation apparent to all. In short, our thinking in trivial matters is being lightheartedly subjectivized, and this in itself might seem unworthy of grave discussion. But the growing scope of the habit of subjective evaluation is a threat to those fundamental principles of objectivity that are built into the doctrine of a meaningful universe purposely made by God. If a great work of art, a heroic deed, or a mighty communal venture must be valued for what they are, and not for how they tickle the fancy or the feelings of onlookers, then, in proportionate degree, the lesser delights of life must be valued similarly.

Watchfulness in this respect is important because the conscious enemies of Christianity undoubtedly have a vested interest in the promulgation of subjectivist and relativist responses to experience which obliterate objective perspectives and purposes. Their propaganda would be less powerful in effect if we were on our guard against lapsing into the fashionable subjectivist and relativist expressions in lighthearted chatter, and still more when passing judgments on religious or moral matters. We need to recover that awareness of the overall reason and purpose of things that is built into the doctrines of Creation and Divine Providence. For if we neglect the rational bulwarks of the Christian faith, we aid and abet those who are consciously striving to make our fellow beings less rational—less concerned with meaning and overall purpose, more engrossed in the immediacies of subjectivist response.

For our contemporaries, by and large, are not yet consciously orientated away from God. In argument with unbelievers or half-believers you are more likely to meet with protests against "institutionalized religion" or against "formalized dogma" or against "ritualized response" than with atheism. This, of course, is because the trend is to retain the idea of God, but to transmute this Being into some kind of spirit that broods over that meaningless flux we have described, a Being who is the antithesis of the divine Architect with a will and a purpose. A God is still wanted by most of our contemporaries, it would seem. What is not wanted is a God with a will, a plan, a purpose—a rational God overlooking an interpretable history. It is perhaps wise to try to make people face this comprehensive issue squarely. The standard protests against institutionalized religion, formalized dogma, and ritualized response generally disguise a deeper objection against the challenge of the supernatural. Attachment to the slogans of self-indulgent subjectivism has the effect of insulating mental laziness.

It can be salutary to reason at the most basic level, whether with others or with oneself. "Very well: let's not beat about the bush. Let us suppose, for purposes of argument, that Christianity is a pack of lies. There is no God, no Savior, no life beyond this life, no point in prayer, worship or saintly self-sacrifice. Every fundamental Christian doctrine is based on delusion. Let us take our starting-point there. What then? What is life all about? Why does the universe exist? Why does man exist?"

Thus challenged, probably most people would be likely to resist hypothetical abolition of the Christian case as rigorously as they would have resisted any defense of dogma or institutionalism. They are likely to put the brake on total demolition: "Hold on. I didn't say that. I didn't mean that. I wouldn't go anything like as far as that. I do believe in God, as a matter of fact." And that is quite a useful starting point for any apologetic. We are suggesting that the Christian apologist, by pushing the anti-Christian case to its logical conclusion, may find his former opponent suddenly leaping over to his side and beginning to reconstruct the faith he set out to destroy.

This suggestion is not made here as a recipe for evangelism. Rather it is intended to illustrate the state of mind we have to deal with today and the need to open up again the path for rational argument from fundamentals. There is no point in trying to justify ecclesiastical institutionalism to an unbeliever who is lost in relativistic subjectivism. But there perhaps is a point in trying to set his mind on the path of natural theology, by going right back to the beginning. God or no God? Doubting the truth of Christianity must be faced in all its implications. The stark alternative to Christianity must be frankly and fully faced. For if Christ was not God, then he was at worst a terrible fraud, at best a madman. As for the question whether God exists or not, it resolves itself basically into acceptance of purpose or chance as a first cause. It is not very easy for any man to look out upon our universe and say "It must have made itself—by accident."

Indeed, if we forget everything the Christian faith has taught us, if we forget the Old and New Testaments, the coming of our Lord, the experience of prayer, the witness of saints and martyrs—if we forget all this and simply look out on the world we live in, we find ourselves admitting that it looks like something consciously and purposefully designed. Things in it belong together. As living creatures we have certain needs and they have been neatly provided for in the world we have been placed in. There is water to drink, food to eat, fuel to keep us warm, materials from which to make shelter, clothing, and all the refinements of civilized life. Either the whole thing is a mighty accident, or else it fulfills some overall purpose. There is no third alternative. The whole universe, with all its inhabitants, has just occurred, just happened, like that—meaninglessly, haphazardly; or else it works out the conscious purpose of a divine Maker. Chance or purpose; these appear to be the only two possibilities. If ours is not an accidentally produced universe, then it is a consciously purposed one; consciously purposed by God; for a being with a conscious purpose and the wisdom to make a universe is certainly a Person and certainly divine. That is why, as Austin Farrar said in that delightful little book, *Saving Belief*, the question "Is God personal?" is such a silly one. As Farrar says, it is like asking "Is ice frozen?" If it isn't frozen, it isn't ice, because that's what we mean by the word "ice." If God isn't personal, he isn't God, because that is what the word "God" means. If you deny that God is personal, you are not starting an argument with traditional theology—nothing so exciting as that; you are engaged in a dispute with the English language. You might like to think you have taken on the Bible, or at least the Creeds; but you have not. You have taken on the Oxford Dictionary.

We look out upon our world and we judge that it expresses the conscious purpose of a divine maker, in that it seems too coherent, too ordered, too dramatic, too packed with hidden and discoverable meanings to be the product of accidental growth. Some people will dispute this and argue: "But the really wonderful things in the world—television and airplanes, computers and space technology, great works of art and literature—are not a God's creation; they are man's." They go to show what a wonderful brain man has and how unlimited is the potential range of his achievement. "What the created universe has given us—coal and wood and iron ore and the like—is really very crude by comparison with what man has made of these things by his skill: rockets and radio, vases and violins." The most obvious reply to this is that man's brain is not his own creation; man did not invent himself. The brain which enables him to make these wonderful things is as much God's gift as the raw materials from which they are made.

William Temple developed this point very interestingly in his book, *Nature, Man and God.* The fact about our universe that is most striking, Temple argued, is not the thing itself—suns and stars, the earth and its produce. Nor is it man, with the remarkable ability that his hands have and his brain, his eyes and his ears. The really striking thing is that when man, with his hands and his senses and his brain, gets to work on this world of ours, with its metals and rubber and coal and wood, then the two things (man and his world) mesh together in such a way that you get all these wonderful products—radio and spacecraft, pianos and cathedrals. It is the meshing together that gives the game away, Temple argued. The world is like a lock; man is like a key. The key fits the lock so exactly that when the one operates on the other the door is opened upon civilization—literature, music, art, and all the things that make life culturally rich.

To say "What a wonderful world this is" is like saying "What a wonderful lock this is." To say "What a wonderful being man is" is like saying "What a wonderful key this is." The balanced response goes further. "How extraordinary! The key fits the lock. It must have been purposely designed for it."

For this reason people are utterly wrong who speak as though advances in science and technology have made the Faith more difficult to accept. Whenever I hear it said in a sermon: "We all find our faith stretched by the great discoveries of the space age," I say to myself, "Not me, for one." Why on earth should anybody's faith be disturbed by the discoveries of the space age? What kind of faith is it that receives a knock when an astronaut lands on the moon? What doctrine is undermined when a piece of man-made machinery hurtles towards Jupiter? What is the hidden connection which some preachers appear to discern between accelerating mobility within space and the teaching of the Church? As a rational being, I am baffled by the claim that anyone's faith can be diminished by new advances in rocketry. Surely new advances in technology should have the very opposite effect, each one making the Christian's faith more secure. The more complicated a thing proves to be, the more complex and subtle the relationship of part with part, the more certain you are that it has been consciously designed and has not occurred by accident. When I first drove a car on which the old manual transmission had been superseded by the syncro-mesh system, my faith in the existence of a conscious manufacturer behind the machine was not in the least shaken. Now that I can buy one with a fully automatic transmission, I do not have to confess that my belief in the conscious operations of a living design team has received a smack in the eye.

Such is the climate of current irrationality that it is perhaps worthwhile to press this point home. A world containing nothing except living trees and plants — might it not, after all, have just happened of its own accord? But a world containing men and women with brains and faculties so finely adjusted to their environment that they can manufacture satellites, transistors, and hi-fi recordings — surely, as G.K. Chesterton observed, the whole thing begins to look like a plot. Let us hear no more of the illogical notion that new scientific discovery can make the Christian's faith less tenable. Every development and invention that shows afresh how complex is the connection between what we human beings can do and the sort of world we inhabit is further evidence that the whole scheme was devised by a mighty Intelligence which makes man's own understanding and skill look slight by comparison.

We see our world as a world consciously planned and directed, a world with a purpose, a world under God. The matters which sometimes gravely worry us as we cling to the faith have nothing to do with wonderful things like scientific advances, which largely uncover and explicate God's design for the world. We are more likely to be troubled in faith by evidence of suffering than by evidence of progress. And indeed the most powerful objection to the Christian case runs something like this: "What about suffering? How can the world be governed by a good God? How can talk about a divinely created world consciously purposed and directed by God be reconciled with all the misery and pain in the world? Maybe plenty of it is due to our own faults and failings — and we could get rid of it if we had a mind to; but there remains a vast mass of suffering that is not at all due to man's neglect or his evil intentions. It is inescapable — cancer and paralysis, sudden disaster and untimely bereavement, deformity from birth and insanity. Talk about a good God has to take account of all the pain and misery in the world he has made."

This apparent contradiciton can trouble people deeply – and so it should. Suffering is a very serious matter and, in a sense, too serious to be bandied about in logical argument, however well-intentioned. But what troubles us here is not that suffering in itself destroys faith (for we have evidence that it is just as likely to strengthen faith) but that the spectacle of suffering shakes the security of non-suffering people in their faith. The reader may think perhaps that I am splitting hairs, but the distinction being made here is a crucial one. Objectors do not generally urge their direct personal experience of pain as evidence against the existence of a good God. Men and women wracked with agony are not shouting out from hospital beds that the notion of a good God is untenable. Rather men and women are sitting in comfort as I sit now, with pens in their hands, and are wondering how they can reconcile the facts of evil and suffering with Christian notions of divine Providence. What we are saying is that, for argumentative purposes, pain is not the problem; rather the *problem* of pain is the problem. That is why we can push the pen smoothly across the paper in a comfortable room and write words like "pain" and "suffering" as easily as one might write "sugar" or "bacon." A fellow being in torment is one thing; and the argument that torment disproves the existence of a good God is another and very different thing.

Actual pain does not allow the luxury of composing treatises for or against the existence of God. Indeed, the deeper the human emergency, the more man's utterance becomes a cry, a prayer – and the less likely it is to formulate a case for or against anything. A good deal of theological argument – especially the kind that questions the fundamentals of the faith – is simply the product of having too much time on one's hands, of having no emergency to deal with, of being remote from the kind of human suffering and human need that cry out for answering strength and comfort. Aberrant theology is the offspring of affluence and ease.

It is generally from situations of personal ease and comfort that the argument is launched that the suffering in the world makes faith in a benevolent God impossible. Thomas Hardy lived into his nineties; he was hale and vigorous, enjoying his three meals a day, taking his train trips to London to be lionized at the dinner parties of the socialites, when he agonized in *The Dynasts* over the wickedness of the "God" who had the heartlessness to subject his human victims to the Napoleonic Wars. *The Dynasts* was not written (like Scott's *The Bride of Lammermoor*) on a bed of pain. It was written in a cosy and handsomely equipped study which you can take a peep into if you visit the museum at Dorchester. There *are* literary and religious works that spring directly from circumstances of extreme privation or distress. Dame Julian of Norwich's exhilarating *Revelations of Divine Love* was the product of self-imprisonment in an anchoress' cell, and Thomas More's sturdy *Dialogue of Comfort and Tribulation* was the product of incarceration in the death cell.

It is necessary to say these things because the writer always feels a kind of effrontery in talking gravely about suffering when sitting in comfort. Whether suffering in practice more often deepens or weakens Christian faith is not something I can pretend to know anything about. But the *problem* of suffering—that is to say, the argument that suffering disproves the existence of a good God—is a theoretical, intellectual thing, and must be examined as such. We approach the reality of suffering with warm hearts—with awe, pity, compassion, help, and relief. We approach the argument that suffering disproves God's existence with clear heads and cool emotions.

Our world is full of odd, unaccountable things, some pleasant, some unpleasant—elephants, jellyfish, music, sunsets, streptococci, dry rot, azaleas, suffering. We start with an incongruous list purposely. These are some of the things life presents to us, some likable, some dislikable. But, of the dislikable things, only suffering is picked out as being an obstacle to belief in God. Nobody says, "I could believe in God if it were not for dry rot." Yet surely, if there is no good God, then suffering is no more remarkable than dry rot. It is unpleasant and dislikable. We should prefer to be without it, as we should prefer to be without Portuguese men-o'-war or rats. A world so designed that it was disfigured by none of the things we find unpleasant would have obvious advantages. But, unless you posit a good God, suffering is just one more of those unaccountable things that occur. An accidental universe, with no good God behind it, has surely just as much reason and right to throw up suffering among its products as it has to throw up kangaroos or jellyfish, or creatures like you and me with two legs, two arms, and a cavity up top in front which opens and shuts on hinges, and into which we throw boiled potatoes and cream buns.

If there is no God, there is nothing remarkable about suffering and therefore its existence does not pose a problem. It is irrational to say "I can't believe in God because of suffering," because without God the existence of suffering is not a problem but only a fact. It becomes a problem—something that needs to be specially explained and accounted for—only when you have accepted that there is a good God at the back of everything. Indeed, if one may so put it, the better the God, the more difficult it seems at first sight to explain why his world should contain so much misery. That is why Christians must always feel especially sympathetic toward those people who say to us, "I can't believe in God, not after what has happened to me or mine—not since my brother was killed in an accident, not since my daughter died of paralysis." People who argue thus are already half-believers in God, or they would not have need to make this protest. Without a basic, instinctive sense of a purposed universe, they would have no cause for indignation. They would accept suffering as the kind of thing to be expected in a world produced by chance. Their protest springs from a deep sense that there should be, ought to be, love and sympathy and conscious purpose at the back of everything, and not blind chance which is indifferent to pain.

Thus the fact that the problem of suffering troubles what we call our faith means that we have, at bottom, accepted that life is not chancy and accidental, but under the governance of a loving God. Suffering troubles us because it cuts across the grain. Across what grain? Suffering troubles us because it does not fit in. Fit in with what? These questions point to the presupposition, in every questioner's mind, in favor of the divine governance which suffering seems to bring into question. The intellectual paradox here is a sharp one. The complaint against suffering is irrational, indeed unutterable, unless there is something to be complained at. A complaint presupposes an offense. Offense against what? The cycle of reasoning repeats itself. What is it that suffering offends against?

Our questions can best be answered by analogy. Suppose you wanted to lay a square patio of crazy paving in your garden. You order a load of broken flagstones. Then you tackle the tricky business of fitting them together. You are not surprised if you are left at the end with two or three pieces which cannot possibly be fitted into the space remaining. You are not surprised, because you never supposed that the broken pieces had been designed to enable you to fill up your square. You have no complaint against your supplier for sending you flagstones which have not properly met your needs.

But suppose you buy a jigsaw puzzle at a shop. You fit it together carefully and intelligently, and at the end you are left with a hole and some pieces that do not fit into it. You are very surprised indeed. You are offended. You have a just complaint against the manufacturers of the puzzle, whereas you had no case against the suppliers of the broken flagstones. For your complaint implies an intention, a conscious design, a purposed pattern — and failure to match up to it.

Suffering does not fit into the scheme of things, we feel. There is no cause for human surprise, indignation, or protest unless the scheme is a conscious scheme designed by a good God. In short, every man who protests against human suffering bears witness that inwardly, at bottom, he has a presupposition in favor of a good God and a divinely created universe, and he has found something that cuts against the grain of that presupposition. Unless we presuppose a good God at the back of the universe, the question "Why suffering?" is on a par with the question "Why cabbages?"

The mysteries of human suffering and of the often teased, never fully satisfied, human search for happiness are closely bound up with the thirst for God. When we spoke earlier of the idolatries which engage and too much engross the mind of modern man, we were concerned with objects and interests to which many turn to appease desires that are not really susceptible of fulfillment within the finite order. Humanism assumes that there is nothing in store for us but what the finite order has to offer. It assumes that the good things of life — education, hospitals, art, music, literature, home comforts, transport and the like—when widely and evenly distributed and enjoyed, will produce the only well-being of which man is capable. Yet the known blessings of life, however fairly distributed, can never be enjoyed with a wholly quiet conscience so long as there is one human being living a life of suffering such as can be brought about by natural or accidental events that human effort is powerless to prevent. Millions of lives lived in comfort and happiness cannot cancel out the reality of a single life of suffering, cannot swamp it quantitatively or dilute it as the sea would dilute a droplet of poison. Besides, supposing that you could produce the most perfectly satisfying state of human existence on earth for all men living (and who imagines that you could?), even then the fact that human beings have already lived in the past lives of misery and suffering would constitute for all time a cause for protest against the injustice of things.

The man of conscience cannot be content that as many people as possible should be as happy as possible on this earth. He does not like the idea of perfect happiness for others and for himself in a world in which there are those who are suffering through no fault of their own. He does not want undisturbed happiness in an earthly life in which innocent people in the past have suffered agony—*unless* those very same people are now experiencing something very different.

If this life is the whole show, the man of conscience rejects it as one vast manifestation of injustice, one vast display of absurdity, if not of evil. If the experience between birth and death constitutes the sum total of the individual's consciousness, then that total consciousness has in many cases been three parts unmerited misery, three parts undeserved pain. Does one want to be happy with a setup in which such is or has been the last word for a single human being? Does one want to enjoy food, music, or friendship in a setup which arbitrarily arranges that fellow creatures across the way, or across the world, shall have a total experience of consciousness which is largely privation, distress, or pain? Of course, *if* their painful experience between birth and death does not represent their total experience of consciousness, if there is something *for them* which reduces this experience to the nature of a phase, which transforms its status to that of the transient, its character to that of the preparatory, then indeed the case is altered.

Notice what is being said. The Christian rejects unbelief because it comes to terms with injustice and inequality; because it presupposes that a setup can be self-explanatory and self-authenticating which has allowed unmerited suffering to dominate individual lives. This is not just a protest against unhappiness; it is a protest against happiness, if that happiness is relished in the context of a total experience which for some is largely compounded of misery. Can the man of conscience endure well-being for himself, the intolerable burden and price of it, except within a total scheme which caters for the correction of injustice and the healing of pain? Such a system, the only kind that could satisfy the human demand for justice, is greater than a finite system and something much more than a haphazard system.

For the human consciousness to study the universe without taking itself into account is an absurdity. The universe is such that a purposeful God must have made it; the human consciousness is such (with its deep rejection of the pain about us in that universe) that a compassionate God must have made it. To take the human consciousness into account is to reckon with rejection of suffering; it is also to reckon with a demand and a hunger which reach out of time, for they can never be fully satisfied by the arbitrary and temporary contingencies of earthly life. To study the universe rationally is to study man too. The universe inhabited by the human consciousness is the thing we have to reckon with, the only universe we know. The human consciousness is in the field, and in the middle of the field, right from the start in an enquiry into the system we are involved in. That human consciousness operates a conceptual equipment capable of fine reckonings and measurements, including indispensable precision tools like the concepts of "cause" and "effect." This equipment makes reasoning possible, enables reasoning to begin. Reasoning therefore cannot lay aside this equipment as unreliable in the middle of argument. Moreover reasoning is dependent not only on the operation of a fine equipment of conceptualization built into the human consciousness; it is also wholly dependent upon the impulse of consciousness which sets the machinery in action. This impulse is the demand for order. Since the demand for order sets reasoning's conceptual equipment in motion, reasoning can scarcely halt itself in midstream to announce that the demand for order is invalid. This is what is known as sawing off the branch on which you are sitting.

Maintaining the human consciousness firmly in the center of the system we inhabit when investigating that system, in effect concedes priority to a conceptual currency and to a motivating demand for order. It also concedes priority to a rationale in terms of which order is worth seeking (as opposed to disorder), meaning is worth having (as opposed to meaninglessness), knowledge is preferable to ignorance, understanding preferable to obscurity, and truth preferable to falsehood. On the maintenance of these massive objectivities the maintenance of rationality depends. The assault upon them, by the forces of subjectivism and relativism, whether in the guise of thought-out treatise or in the form of the thoughtless chatter of semi-literate trendies, is corrosive of the Christian mind.